"Arrive At Success :: Conversations Between Networkers That Could Tell Lots About Your Future" is a novel that takes the reader into the psyche of a successful networker.

It goes behind the scenes into the world of network marketing... and in a gripping narrative style reveals the connections with higher consciousness, which even most insiders of this industry never reach.

This book is a must-read for anyone looking at businesses of the 21st century with any amount of seriousness. Some of the author's experiences could impact your mind once and forever.

Written to be read and re-read, Arrive At Success is a treat with inspiring stories, quotable quotes, quips and usable one-liners. But more than that, it is a practical guide for development of consciousness to pave the way for eventual success.

D'claimer

This claimer claims that all people referred to and written about in this book are real and can be seen, heard and felt (tasting and smelling are optional). The purpose of this claimer is to assert that Network Marketing is a very 'real' industry and anyone associating with it is associating with a future that only few have yet seen and understood. Everyone who has experienced success with it will have no issues in identifying with the industry as it has impacted their lives in ways unexpected of any other human endeavor. The places, events and conversations are fictional however.

Sandeep Nath

Note: All persons mentioned in this book have been sent advance copies of the book for review. None have objected to the use of their name. Several have sent in reviews, quoted here. All brands and trademarks mentioned are owned by their respective entities.

"I loved the storytelling style. You can read through again and again to discover something new every time"

- *Norbert Orlewicz, Owner MLSP*

"Sandeep Nath has opened up a Pandora's box with this book. His ideas are not just relevant, they are in fact required for the new age human being. His book can best be explicated as 'a road map to Spiritual Capitalism'. A must read for anyone at any stage in life"

- *Arjun Aiyar, Owner thinQ dynamiQ*

"Arrive At Success has a lot of depth. Many points hit home squarely and need to be understood in their multiple dimensions before they are imminently quoted"

- *Basant Panday, Owner IndiaLog*

"Sandeep has crafted a lifetime of lessons into one captivating story. You get caught up in the journey and you don't realize you are learning. So it would pay to read it a second time with highlighter in hand so you don't miss the important life lessons."

- *Dean McNamara, Owner NZMarketingSystems.com*

"You have made us to understand how to be responsible for our thoughts and actions; you become empowered to make choices that lead to balance and fulfillment. You have taken a torch of a new higher consciousness way to do things… and I will follow you in this great endeavor."

- *Roger Aburto, World Superhuman Project*

"Take the Wisdom of Deepak Chopra, The Insight of Anthony Robbins and the Teaching of Robert Kiyosaki, mix it with astute observation and personal experience and you have an awesome read to improve your own personal philosophy – well done Sandeep"

- Sam Star, Teacher & Global Entrepreneur

"Why don't people understand networking? Sandeep has discovered the solution. It takes both time and experience to absorb this concept. Sandeep takes his readers with him on his personal journey in search of discovering what networking is. Through his storytelling manner he captures his readers attention long enough so they can start to understand the networking concept. The book is outstanding and at the end of his book you want to turn it back over and start to immediately reading it again."

- Sue DeBrule, Author of Rise Above The Rat Race

"Here are principles that will help you grow, not only in business but in life. Sandeep has put it all together in this well written treatise. No networker should be without this book."

- Doug Wead, New York Times bestselling author, adviser to two American Presidents, network marketer and historian

Acknowledgements

Thanks Energy. Period.

Preamble

This book carries many references to the B-quadrant. This is the B-quadrant as defined by Robert Kiyosaki, first in his book Cashflow Quadrant. He assigns it to a 'way of thinking'. He says there are 4 ways to live life as defined by our thinking.

The 'E-quadrant' is of the 'Employee' who has a job. The 'S-quadrant' is of self-employed persons who have businesses or are professionally engaged. Both these quadrants operate on an exchange of time for money... making the person's physical presence critical,  while the work is done for someone else's system. Income is generated 'actively' (when the person stops, income stops).

Then we have the right quadrants. The 'B-quadrant' where 'Business owners' own and operate a System. And the 'I-quadrant' where 'Investors' invest money in systems. In the right quadrants the system / money works for its people. Income for the people here is thus generated 'passively' (income does not stop even when the person is away).

For example, as an author I could work in the S-quadrant, writing and selling my books. Or I could plug into the publishing 'System' and let a royalty income come to me.

Another example. McDonald's is a System (B-quadrant) to make burgers and it probably sells more burgers in one city than all the hamburger stands (S-quadrant) put together all over the world. The System works for the McDonald's owner and his income is 'passive'. Contrast this with the burger stand owner who could even work 15 hours a day, but his income would always be 'active'.

Now the question is, would most people prefer to have an active income or a passive income? Then why are most people (90%+) in the left quadrants? And why is most of the world's wealth (90%+) controlled by the few in the right quadrants? The answer is Education. Most of us do not get educated by (or stay in the company of) B-quadrant people.

Why? Because we just don't know that we can. We think we must earn and live our lives based on the education we received in school. The right quadrants are risky, we think.

This is, in fact, not true. On the contrary, since there are fewer people – and an abundance of wealth – on the right side, many people on the right are very willing to mentor people who choose to switch.

Robert Kiyosaki says, "Poor people (left quadrants) work; Rich people (right side) network." Just like we learn to work, we need to learn to network. This is what makes successful network marketers exemplary B-quadrant people.

Many of them you shall meet in the following pages…

- ❧ -

The B-quadrant stands for 'abundance' (as opposed to limiting beliefs) and 'collaboration' (as opposed to competition), as it holds more money and less people. The distribution ratio between the left and right quadrants is badly skewed today… but even as it moves from 90:10 to 80:20, the world will be impacted like no other social change.

- ❧ -

\- ✎ -

As long as you're working for money, you're in a rat race. Once you have a system work for you, you rise above it… that is life in the B-quadrant.

- from 'Rise Above The Rat Race' *by Sue DeBrule*

\- ✎ -

Nama took me completely by surprise

"Congratulations Sandeep, with what you've just told me, you are a fully qualified member of the Leader's Club... you're halfway to diamond!"

"Huh.. uh ... thanks!" I offered with a weak smile.

For the life of me I couldn't figure that one out. I had been hanging out with these guys since just a few weeks... and often I had heard them tell me that getting to diamond was a two to five-year journey... that was the pinnacle of achievement for networkers in general... so how could I already be halfway to diamond? Was I really that smart?

"Here, Arjun asked me to let you have these very special tapes when you crack LC." That was Tharini, Nama's wife, pulling up from beside the big man, with a bundle of what seemed to be a dozen or so tapes. "Congratulations!" she exclaimed, extending her short enthusiastic hand that seemed to flutter with the whim of her smile.

"Huh.. uh ... thanks! But what's all this about Tharini? All I said was that Asiya has signed up on the continuing education program..." I repeated, wondering what could have got them so excited about this 'halfway to diamond' thing. Yes, Mahesh had been goading me on to finish that signup so I qualify for 'Leader's Club' (or LC)… but the rest of the excitement went beyond me.

Nama smiled. Nama is a guy who handled a team of about 1500 people at his job. The 'Most Effective' Vice President of his company the previous year. The only thing Nama said he knew, over and above what the other VPs did, were the B-quadrant leadership principles our mentors taught and applied. How to smile the way he did was one of them.

The ability to answer inane questions repeatedly with a patient smile was another. I was really bringing out his full potential! "A diamond just does what you did. You've done the LC module yourself. Now you know everything you need to 'know'. Now you just have to 'do'."

The words 'know' and 'do' were deliberately emphasized. At least in India many people have knowledge but very few apply it. Was he ensuring I sensitize myself to it?

Mahesh was overhearing our conversation and chipped in, "Yes Sandeep, diamond is just about enabling others to go LC. About 50 others. That's all."

50 others. That's all? Hmmm… if I did LC in a month, 50 would mean 50 months. That's the two to five years these guys talk about. And I now have the skills one needs to get there. Now I have to empower others. Hmmm… seemed to make sense.

"Please keep your mobile phones in silent mode. We know your calls are important but so is this meeting." "Uh." My thoughts were abruptly interrupted by this announcement. Mahesh and I were entering a meeting hall when Nama and

Tharini had intercepted us. It was a meeting of our network marketing team. My first 'big meeting' as an insider.

I felt Nama tap my shoulder, "Right Sandeep, see you after the meeting." Saying so, smiling characteristically, he sped off with Tharini and Mahesh to the front of the hall. I found a place and continued my wonder.

"These are a strange bunch of guys." Here I was, all by myself, tapes in hand, waiting for some strange meeting to start. There was music… people danced about in the open space around the central aisle. There was noise… no, cacophony. Come to think of it, it was actually a very festive atmosphere. People looked happy. Not everyone seemed rich… but were surely well to do… some stretching their means. The stretch-types seemed to make up for their appearance through the brightness in their eyes. Everyone looked extremely positive. Who are these guys? They didn't look like salesmen.

Well, I was not a salesman either. I was a brand consultant. Mahesh was an electronics store-chain owner. Nama was a cost accountant who headed an outsourcing division. What was there to sell anyway? Again my thoughts were interrupted. It was the national anthem. Everyone fell silent. We rose.

After the anthem, about half the hall clapped. I didn't. I asked my neighbor who did, "is it ok to clap after the anthem?"

"Clapping keeps you excited," he said. "Any harm in staying excited all your life?" Sound logic, I thought.

"Ladies and Gentlemen, welcome… I'm Dr. Sudhakar Reddy and I will be your host for this fine Sunday morning. You are here at a Business Building Seminar or BBS, which we actually consider a Brain Building Seminar. The business we are in looks obvious but it is not. It's simple… but is also as complex as we are. And though it comes in an ugly-looking brown paper bag… it is solid gold inside. How much of this gold can you uncover for your family's security? It is only limited by how much of your brain you can develop. And for this, I am delighted to present to you today's speaker…" And his voice trailed off in my consciousness because I stayed on with the 'brain building seminar' phrase he used.

For quite a while I didn't hear anything else. It happens with all of us. We stop at some word and stay with it. Missing the moments as they go along. If only we could tune into each and every moment of our lives… we would live so fully and grow so much more.

Like the story of the Zen monk and his disciple. They were walking through the forest when they came upon a stream. A young woman was trying to negotiate getting across, but the slippery rocks didn't agree with her footwear. Just then the mentor said, "Don't bother Madam, I will carry you across." And saying so, he did. Once they were by themselves on the other side, the younger monk couldn't contain himself and burst out, "Master! What did you do! Zen prohibits us from mingling with women and carrying them around is blasphemy! How could you possibly do that?" And the master replied, "Son I merely helped a fellow spirit across the stream. You are the one who's carrying a woman in your mind all this while."

That, is what being in the NOW is about. That is what living as a spiritual being with a human experience is truly. We are so caught up in looking upon ourselves as human beings with spiritual experiences… spirituality is really the reverse. Oneness lies in being one with the spiritual form always… and yet conducting ourselves in the human form, doing whatever might be required to be done at that moment.

I suddenly realized I'd moved into a different thought stream altogether sparked by the brain-building phrase. Shaking myself back in, I found there was a lot in this environment that I never found in the corporate world. And it all seemed good. Just sitting there absorbing the stray words that came into my brain, I felt I was growing. Brain building. Hmmm…

Just then Mahesh came into focus. He was walking up to me somewhat hurriedly.

"You're next." "Next??" And sure enough, there was an announcement… "All new leader's clubs since the last BBS please come up on the stage." Unsure of what I was getting into, I got up and got onto the stage. Ten or so others were around me. "Congratulations!" said the MC, "please state your name, occupation and one line why you're onto this project."

"Aseem and Puja Grover. Mechanical Engineer in the auto sector. I want to be free from my job, become a consultant, and spend all my time with my wife and two-year old son." "Jayant and Mahi Vashist. Chartered Accountants. We have been practicing 15 years and have not been able to take a single vacation. We want to travel the world." There were another couple of couples. I meandered my way to the last.

"Sandeep Nath. I run a consulting company and I want to learn how to build a system based business." There were claps. Lots of claps as we stepped off the stage. Now what are they excited about, I wondered.

Just then I caught sight of Nama and Tharini. He hugged me and she had an ear-to-ear smile. Naturally, it reflected. I was all smiles. All charged. All confused… and all confident. Mahesh shook my hand. The meeting resumed. I felt two inches taller.

I don't remember who the speaker was, but I remember he was introduced as a phenomenal speaker with businesses across continents. Owning large businesses had been my dream too, and that's why that left a strong impression. I also remember he told us an incredible story. Of Hernando Cortez.

Now Mr Cortez was an infamous conqueror, who in 1519 took it into his head that he would take 11 ships, 500 soldiers, 100 sailors, and 16 horses from Spain to Mexico. Why? There was a huge treasure that lay there, guarded by the Mayans since hundreds of years. Numerous conquerors had died in earlier attempts to get it. But the treasure was real and Cortez realized he would need people of extraordinary commitment to accompany him on this voyage.

So, for starters, Cortez did not just recruit the people to go with him. He laid a vision out for them. He spoke to each family about how great their future would be as they returned with the treasure. He built the dream of how their generations would live in wealth and favor… and the right people came on board.

When they landed on the shore, again he did not immediately embark on the conquest. He laid everyone down on the beach and they shared. They shared the belief that they would go back to their happy families with the riches. They immersed in the thoughts of running their hands through the jewels and the diamonds and the gold and imprinted that deep into their minds.

And finally, the day came when Cortez would tell them the strategy. The brass-tacks. And everyone gathered around expecting directions on who would do what and who would cover whom and etc. But Cortez did none of that. He just said 3 words. 3 decisive words, that in one stroke sealed the fate of their voyage. 3 words that ensured they would not perish like the earlier speculators. 3 words that made the decision. And those 3 words were, "Burn the ships." If they were going home, they were going home in the Mayan ships. No options!

Burn the ships. What a concept! Burn the ships. What were my ships I wondered? What did I run back to, every time the going got tough? What really limited my potential?

By now, sitting by myself in the hall, I was coming into consciousness of my dream as well. I wanted to have businesses all over the world. I had always wanted that. I just didn't know how. IIT did not teach me that. Neither did IIM. All they did was made me an expert. And an expert is stuck to his place. Trading his time for money. An expert has no leverage. He is not a B-quadrant guy. And so an expert's dreams are restrained by what he can do with his own time and money. Which is why, all I could think of – to say from stage – was, "I want to learn how to build a system based business." I didn't say I wanted to build an international business. I didn't even say I wanted to travel the world. I just said what my analytical mind told me I was permitted to dream.

In fact I didn't even believe that this mickey-mouse operation could result in anything very substantial. Even though the speaker has already walked the path. Even though my own sponsor, Mahesh Raju had.

The fact was, I didn't know anything about 'heart'.

"The left quadrants are driven by head Sandeep. The B-quadrant is driven by heart," Mahesh had explained casually while telling me his growth story. And now he was with me again as we were walking back to our cars. "How did you feel about the LC recognition?" he asked.

"I felt great. I had not expected this."

Mahesh smiled. "Hold that feeling. Program your mind to recall it for you whenever you feel otherwise. This meeting has served you well – for life! Now you must finish your bookings for Malaysia."

Mahesh's timing was perfect. At every meeting, book the next one. And your activity will move flawlessly.

Basil Harris, our mentor in Australia, was coming to Malaysia. He was calling his Indian, Singaporean and Thai teams to Johar Baru (JB, Malaysia) for an LC-and-up qualification meet. "And yes, this meeting will be very important for you to imbibe the system," Mahesh continued.

He always chose his words carefully. Another learned skill of network marketing. 'For you to imbibe the system' he said. Not for you to go diamond. Not for you to be free. Not for you to have an international business. Just for you to imbibe the system. Just what I was looking for. Who else but my upline knew me that well?

"It really is a mickey-mouse business you know. Malaysia will show you that." We laughed. It was a joke we both knew. Mickey Mouse was one of the largest entertainment businesses of our times… appreciating that was a matter of perspective.

*****

"I am happy you made it." Nama had his standard clichés but they still sounded nice. Especially after an overnight flight to JB. And I reflected that no one else in my life took the trouble to articulate such words. My wife certainly did not. She hadn't come with me to Malaysia either. She didn't share my dream. She didn't bother with these people. But she still loved me dearly, however strangely she might have shown it.

"Arjun came in last night", continued Nama as he led me into his room. We hadn't been able to get the same connection from India so Tharini and Nama had preceded my arrival and checked in a few hours earlier.

It was a classy hotel. We took rooms in it so the conference could be residential in nature. One wall of Nama's room overlooked a sprawling lawn, lush with tropical greenery, recently washed in early summer rain. I took a place in the corner of the room so I would not be distracted by the magnificence of nature and could focus on what he had to tell me about Arjun.

All I knew was, Arjun was his upline; a 32 year old karate black belt who had been financially free since six years. He'd worked 3 years at a famous multinational bank in Mumbai after his MBA, but his freedom was far too precious for him to want to continue... and network marketing had been his escape route... in spite of a 9 to 9 job. As a management student he had had the good fortune of coming under the tutelage of Basil Harris in Australia. And he'd followed Basil's footsteps - and the B-quadrant training system - to be free and stay free ever since. He was younger than all of us. And richer than most of us. Very sharp. Very confident. Very humane. He confessed to me later that he hadn't always been like that. "This business teaches you life," he'd mentioned in passing, with a naughty wink.

But Nama was excited too, to be in the midst of people even he had only just heard about till then. "Sam Star is also here Sandeep", he gushed! "He is quite a talented guy... a versatile actor, trainer, ex-corporate executive... he's 'fun' in human form." Sam was also on Basil's team, in JB from Australia.

"That's too good Nama... I have heard Sam Star on an audio tape earlier. 'Self image and goals' was its title... in fact I've heard this tape about 15 times or more."

"15 times? You're not serious!" Nama screeched playfully. He knew that 15 was the norm for any serious player in the network marketing industry. And this confirmed to him that I was one.

"Nama, Sam touched two areas very dear to me. One was my own self-image. You know I am a page-3 type of person, and I was very concerned about true and false imagery. His talk helped me resolve that."

"Hmmm, and the other?" By now Nama had finished putting his clothes in the cupboard and was looking out of the magnetic window, which had been further magnetized by Tharini's presence in the garden. Would he at all be listening to me, I wondered.

"The other was a story he narrated," I continued, reveling in it myself. "It was of the border area between two of the fragmented east European nations. Evidently they were at peace but the snipers would often take pot shots at each other to entertain themselves. And keep the medicos busy. At other times they'd stroll past the border post and exchange cigarettes or booze. And during one such friendly exchange, one of the soldiers shared the marketing plan. And it went over the border... are you with me?" I paused to check.

"Absolutely! And as I remember it, the business grew and grew and grew thanks to the system. And when there was a call to arms, the soldiers wouldn't shoot at each other, right?" smiled Nama.

"Bingo! Because they represented teams that were creating wealth together... Why would anyone shoot a brother who was at the post only for a few days... set to retire beside the lake with his family thanks to his passive networking income?"

That ignited Nama's mind all right. Jumping into a chair beside me he flipped a few things around on the side table as though he was searching for a paper to write on. Sensing that, I reached for my pocket and pulled out the airline ticket which was one-side printed. He grabbed it with a sparkle in his eye.

Laying it on the table, Nama said, "Sandeep I don't know to this day if Sam's story is real or made-up, but I can see it as real." Nama drew what seemed to be a map with two countries on it. And then a body of soldiers and laypeople on either side. And then, with a frenzy, he began to draw lines across the border and within each country, to depict how people who understood the marketing plan would network with each other just so their sons and daughters... the soldiers... would develop an income source that would take care or them in death or retirement.

"See Sandeep, people across borders want the same things. They want their families close to them, peace, and money to live comfortably. They just have to understand that network marketing is providing all of this through its simple plan," he said, looking towards me for a reaction.

"I can see the peace that network marketing can create. And the camaraderie for personal growth is serious. I've experienced that energy in the atmosphere at my first meeting itself boss," I avered.

Happy with the response, Nama continued, "And you know what I believe? I believe spiritual organizations that seek to support their monks and students will also embrace network marketing as part of their lives very very soon."

"Why is that?" I asked, genuinely baffled by the connection.

"Two reasons at least," Nama said without a blink, "one, because they otherwise scramble about for sponsorships to run their institutions… that's a waste of time and energy… and the money is lying on the table once they network together with their families and town-dwellers. They just need to understand that." He paused to let it sink in. "And two, because as you will soon see, successful network marketers and spiritually elevated beings are on the same wavelength!"

The love. Affection. Trust. Hope. Faith. I had experienced these first-hand. "Successful people in network marketing operate at a higher vibration and that's infectious, isn't it" I asked, knowing the answer already.

And humbly he said, "It is! So shall we go downstairs and meet them?"

The two days of the conference just whizzed past. So much sharing. So much knowledge on relationships, discipline, work ethic and specific issues. Wow! And so much recognition. Happiness. Bliss. It was overwhelming!

The one thing of Malaysia I will carry with me for life will be the sight of new emeralds and new diamonds recognized there. Single burka-clad women literally jumping, screaming whistling on stage. Celebrating freedom from the bottom of their hearts. Connected as one being… from body to mind to emotion, thought and spirit. Vibrating in oneness. Burka, veil and all. Dancing. Ecstatic. Free. Not one, not two, but dozens. Dozens of frenzied women who knew – like Arjun and Cortez – that there was no looking back. And what was behind was very humble anyway. Most often it was a one-room tenement and six kids. And a resolve to change things through a vehicle called network marketing and a mentor.

These ladies shook me up. I imagined such ladies would also be in Pakistan. Such aspiration... such energy existed everywhere. Nobody had yet tapped such enormous human potential and resolve. Our business had not even entered that part of the world. But it would. Maybe from the border. Maybe from the convention halls. I didn't know. All I knew was someone would be needed to plant the seeds. And that someone would be me. A decision was made. A real dream was born. Post-Johar Baru I was a changed man.

Through the trip I learned more about Basil. A former tycoon of South Africa, he was forced to restart life at 37... moving to Australia due to the uncertain business climate back home. He knew nobody – except a close circle of new acquaintances. And they shared the network marketing principles with him.

Using that vehicle Basil, Leone, and their 2 kids under 10, settled into their freedom in 38 months. It had been 29 years since then, and their growth had been continuous. With or without their active involvement. Of course, they had always been involved with mentoring. Passionately. Basil's focus had always been on relationships. He understood early on that network marketing was fundamentally a people activity. And if you can get this one people-activity right, you will get every other people-activity right.

Nama leveraged those very principles to manage the large team of young outsourcers at his workplace. Mahesh built 40 stores for his electronics retail business; that's 40 teams of people working on a shared vision. In their company I quickly learned that network marketing was not a business actually. It was a way of life.

*****

"If you can get this one people-activity right, you will get every other people-activity right. Networking is not something you 'do'. It is something you 'be'."

— Sandeep Nath

*****

In the late nineteen-eighties, Basil, Leone and a handful of diamonds from a few countries teamed up with Jim Dornan to form the system for training people in professional networking. Jim was an extraordinary visionary. With his wife Nancy, he transferred their vision to many across the planet and taught common folk like me to become visionaries. The couple was enormously duplicated and they stand at the pinnacle of vision building. But it wasn't always that way for them either.

Jim and Nancy started their business to explore personal freedom. To have a 20-hour work-week. And they enjoyed exactly that kind of life for a few years. But a financial tsunami struck with the birth of their second child, Eric. This little soul needed a dozen surgeries in his first year just to survive a congenital condition of spina bifida. Medical bills drove them to explore the ceiling on their little network marketing business. And they didn't find any!

30 years later their business has grown to billions of dollars. Eric did good. And thanks to their inclination to invest their time and money on it, the game of 'power-soccer' (played by the likes of Eric on wheelchairs) came to be recognized as an international sport.

"They continue to mentor and influence lives directly and indirectly. Their significance is felt across entire villages in Africa where they are taking care of AIDS orphans, and in India where they've set up the largest school for resettling street children. Besides this they are lighting up lives with their many books, talks and snippets on leadership, attitude and courage," an introductory note read.

I didn't know any of this when I started. I never could even have guessed. All I knew was, I would explore. And let the skeptic in me rest for a while. And boy, have I been grateful!

Karma

In spite of the perspective I had after the conference in Johar Baru (JB), my audacity and ego blew a lot of potentially good networkers out of the window. I attribute that to bad karma. Karma that had started many years before I embraced the business myself... with my younger sister!

When she had got introduced to network marketing and wanted me in, she was at college and I was already an established brand consultant. I knew all about the psychology of human behavior and how people are brainwashed (at meetings) to believe they can achieve things extraordinary. And I let her know that without mincing words. But she took it well... she was stronger than most newbies. And though she went on to build quite a substantial network, it was only later when she could was displaced from her peer group that she quit. But by disparaging her I had already earned my bad karma.

Cut back to post-JB. We were at Nama's place. It was a Sunday afternoon. There was a dampness in the air with the monsoon in full fervor, but the mood inside the room was still chirpy. My results were damp too, but the spirit was chirpy thanks to the company it had now started to keep. The discussion was on motivation and that had reminded me of my sister. Dreams, after all, form the foundation of the B-quadrant. "Are you motivated by your dream or by your nightmare?" he'd asked. Either worked, it seemed!

On the white board at one corner of the crowded room were two words; Internal and External. Internal and external motivation, which most people were confused about. Why would anyone take the trouble of building a network? That was the moot point Nandkumar had aired. And Nama had replied with Zen-like terseness, "the answer will come to you when you attend meetings."

It was only in Malaysia that I learned that these meetings do not serve to preach… they serve to awaken. They don't add fuel to the fire… they are the fire. And this self-awakening is what internal motivation is about. What pursuing one's dream is about.

Ever since that trip I had even started to look upon the corporate world differently. The phrase 'all fired up' had started connoting a 'burn-out syndrome'. One that made people run like headless chicken – very fast in circles. Their motivation to do so was generally a paycheck. Or social conformity. Their bigger picture did not arise from any internal fire. One could say their driving motivation was just to chase security or simply conform, rather than truly pursue their larger dreams.

Meanwhile, I was observing the B-quadrant business owners with new eyes. I found they were the truly fired up people, and were actually most calm and relaxed. Like the calm, invisible flame under the vessel of boiling water… it changes the state of water from liquid to gas. Turns the gross to the subtle. That's what these people did. They manifested change inside and around them. B-quadrants were true networkers who harnessed their internal motivation in all aspects of life.

"So anything that motivates us externally is short-lived, right?" said Lakshmi trying to sum up what had been coming.

"Yes, unless it makes us think, it is non-defining for our life", replied Nama. "Most people die without knowing they could have lived differently. That they could have impacted the world."

"Unless they happen to be at a few of our meetings..." someone added as an afterthought.

"These meetings stir us from inside and help us identify our internal motivating factors", I found myself collaborating.

"Yes, that's what makes them critical. Meetings help us understand ourselves better... and our purpose as leaders is to expose our teams to them. Remember your network is only as large as the number of people at your last meeting. And be warned, this can be a very humbling statistic." Nama was frankness unadulterated.

Just then Tharini announced tea and it seemed the right time for a break. As it was, I was counting my group at that meeting and starting to feel depressed. Great ego-killers, these meetings!

I had some official work to catch up with immediately after the meeting and so I excused myself and hopped across to meet Sanjeev. He had an interesting comment on this.

Sanjeev was an extremely well read man and I had briefly partnered with him to grow my consulting practice. He had mentioned he wanted to understand what I did with network marketing and I was excited to tell him. He'd joined immediately. And did not attend a single meeting. He did not understand a thing therefore. Purpose defeated. I always believed he had great potential. But this was his karmic issue.

Like many who quit networking without understanding it, his job too, in this life, had been to preach. Not practice. He could quote economists on the effects of mass social change and the twenty-one factors that drove visionaries. He could talk on the collective unification of purpose. Recite biographies of Hitler. Mussolini. Stalin. But he couldn't fathom distributed purpose and collective responsibility. How each person could be fighting their own demons… to achieve their own personal dreams in a collective, cooperative manner.

"It doesn't happen that way Sandeep", he declared that afternoon.

"It started happening about 75 years ago Sanjeev. Revolutions typically take about a century to bear fruit."

"Are any economists advocating network marketing?"

"I'm sure they are," I said somewhat tentatively. Much after this dialog I learned that Russia had grown tremendously in network marketing, and over 50 post-doctorate economists were involved at a diamond-and-above level. If only I had known and could've quoted this to him then… karma.

"The model is a ponzi scheme", he continued.

"Suit yourself buddy." This attitude of many like Sanjeev told me lots about their approach to life in general. And helped me conclude that network marketing is the greatest filter of human consciousness. Only the ones ready for a higher level of vibration make it here. For they are the ones with influence and impact.

It was incredible the way the universe had put across a few people to me who guided me to this conclusion. Robert Kiyosaki was the first. The B-quadrant was an eye-opener. And its linkages with abundance thinking were shocking. When you put aside your personal intellect you allow yourself to open into divine intelligence it is amazing how easily you transition from the S-quadrant to the B-quadrant of business. Due to this divinity, you operate with untold power.

Power that Sanjeev was clearly not ready for. And in a few months we parted ways.

The 21st century however, is about this radical social change. Through kinesiological studies, Dr. David Hawkins has revealed a very significant aspect of this. He has demonstrated that we operate on a set vibratory scale that determines our responses to any stimulus. At a vibratory level of 25 we perceive guilt in any situation and therefore react accordingly. At a level of 600 we view peace in the very same situation and that would guide how we respond.

It's interesting to note the words 'react' and 'respond'. We mess up our lives by reacting… for that is acting upon impulse. We do not allow our action to receive the benefit of any possible divine intervention – that could come from the part resident in our subconscious. When we respond however, we process the input for a few seconds. Maybe we take a deep breath in the meanwhile. And what we output as a consequence has a greater impact. It's these small deep breaths, small gestures, small practices that cause a big impact on our life and business in the B-quadrant.

Coming back to the vibrations, there was this Peanuts' strip where Charlie Brown (smiling peacefully) picked up a pebble and threw it into a lake. Lucy came charging from behind and screamed, "What did you do! Don't you realize that stone took 3 million years just to get to the shore!" "Good grief." Charlie Brown turned guilty as ever. And it was Lucy's low vibration, driven by anger / jealousy that impacted it.

While we might laugh this off, this really is how we create increasing negativity in society. Which is growing at a frenetic pace thanks to TV. The news has a quality of spreading the bad stuff really fast. And at a low vibration we become magnets of bad stuff. This is why network marketers, preachers and success gurus (like Tony Robbins and Bob Proctor among others) advise strongly against the newspaper and TV. "What we need to know comes to us," they assert.

At a higher vibratory level one only catches the beneficial bits and divinity reaches them across. For instance, I had been the reader of the Times Of India since my school days, but it was only after I came under the positive influence of network marketing that I noticed that the same newspaper had a 'Sacred space' and a 'Quotations' section… most of which made enormous sense and often truly made my day! Here are some great quotes to reflect on.

No one can whistle a symphony. It takes a whole orchestra to play it.
~H.E. Luccock

One piece of log creates a small fire, adequate to warm you up, add just
a few more pieces to blast an immense bonfire, large enough to warm up
your entire circle of friends; needless to say that individuality counts but
team work dynamites. ~Jin Kwon

Coming together is a beginning. Keeping together is progress.
Working together is success. ~Henry Ford

Success is the ability to go from failure to failure without losing your
enthusiasm. ~Winston Churchill

The way these people speak of teamwork, purpose and
collaboration, who can imagine they are referring to
anything other than network marketing? But that's the
beauty of it. Network marketing is life at a higher vibratory
level. It is the springboard for personal success and a
designer life. And what's more, it provides a platform for us
to design other's lives.

Quoting Dr. Hawkins, 'The critical point on the scale is the
200 mark. At less than 200 a person's main concern is
personal survival and they tend to take more out of the
system than they put in. Someone above the 200 mark is
more likely to begin to consider the welfare of others as well
as his or her own. The vast majority of the world's
population is well below the 200 mark. However, because
the few people vibrating at very high levels (500+) are
counteracting the energy of the majority vibrating below
200, the average is 207. Only in the last decade has it passed
the 200 mark. Someone vibrating at around 350 is
counteracting 200,000 people below 200. Someone vibrating

at the level of 500 is counteracting 750,000 people below 200.'

This is what is really exciting. Network marketing will help create a critical mass above 500. Everyone who has achieved any significant level (like 'diamond' and above) does come across really high on energy and positivity. They do love everyone (Love is the state at vibratory level 500). And they have also touched over 200,000 people directly or indirectly.

So this really is a small socio-economic awakening today. A blip on the radar of humanity. But it's significant. Like its people. Not just successful; significant.

Every successful networker is significant because he vibrates at the consciousness that allows him to carry a team of a few 100,000 people towards their dreams. That's collective responsibility for distributed vision. That's the selfless conduct of a life that pays forward. A B-quadrant approach to life dipped in abundance and fuelled by the higher vibrations of human existence (see appendix 1)!

Dr. David Schwartz was another such man who stepped into my life with his book, 'The Magic of Thinking Big'. Here he diagnoses 'Excusitis' as the #1 disease that plagues humanity. What a concept! Further, he writes about Vision. Visualization. Goals. All for the common man. For anyone to achieve. There are many such books… as they say, 'when you take the turn, the scenery changes'.

I took many turns. In fact for a while my life and business were practically going around in circles. But it seemed fun. What I could grasp only much later was that these circles were spiraling upwards. No evident change but lots of growth in a different dimension. And that dimension was spirituality.

The reason spirituality is more in vogue than religion (a quick dipstick on Facebook preferences will validate this statement) is because the old paradigm of iconic religious texts, idols and persona are being replaced by energy shifts. And quantum physicists have also got a handle on this now. It was always evident to Reiki masters and Pranic healers… but today ordinary people like me are becoming energy channels, which are drawn from divine masters in constant connection with the brighter world.

Some of these masters I have personally experienced. Sai Baba, Amma-Bhagwan, Sri Sri Ravi Shankar, Chariji. Equally admirable are the many others who have evolved systems that empower others to enable self-realization through modular teaching packages. I encountered Colin Tipping and Louise Hay through Antharyami; an awakening institute. Bijan was my client. James Redfield, Bob Proctor, Laura Silva, Joe Vitale, Tony Robbins and John Assaraf came to me through various media; books, seminars, courses and programs. All of them are of evolved consciousness and play an active role in furthering the evolution.

And of course, a special mention is due for Jim Dornan. When I first encountered network marketing in the mid-nineties (then mostly multi-level marketing or MLM), I was appalled and cheesed off by the way people almost deified their uplines. Now I understand. It's a low vibration response to a high vibration being. The job of the high vibration being is to create the charge for enhanced consciousness. With Jim, work has always been in progress.

"So what will network marketing do in such a context?" I was intellectualizing with Nama (a highly evolved spiritual being himself) the next day as I carried my thoughts over.

"It will empower", he said, "because leaders empower and network marketing is all about creating leadership."

"And it does not require a management degree to become a leader", I mused.

Nama laughed, "that usually gets in the way!" I knew he wasn't taking a dig at me but I felt miffed anyway. And then I realized I was in awareness of how I felt. Which meant I was better connected to divine awareness. And I felt better.

We were meeting after work at a coffee shop to plan the week. With all the thoughts connecting consciousness with network marketing in my head, I had been silent for most part of the day. My wife had not even noticed, but that too was ok. Any explanation would be like one of the fabled six blind men describing the elephant. The subject was like that. No wonder it took about 6 exposures for an average person to begin to 'get it'.

"Cappuccino?" "That's for him", I said, happy to distract myself again. The waiter placed the iced tea before me and left.

"As long as you can continue to understand the other person Sandeep you will be connected with the other person. "Network marketing is a great practice-field to live life", Nama remarked, continuing the thought.

Hmmm. I didn't really know what to say. All of a sudden the tall tea glass before me seemed to develop a life of its own and briskly swept itself off the table and through my fingers onto the floor. "Oh gosh!"

Without missing a beat Nama said, "we always create our circumstances. The glass reflects your state of confusion about where to land. On the management side or in the leadership stream." He smiled. Always smile when you say anything potentially offensive. "By the same token, you can change everything anytime." Hey, that was the same thing the Antharyami discourse had said out of Colin Tipping's book. Things seemed to be converging again.

"Meditate on it. The answers will come from inside" offered Nama with a smile. Was that a network marketer telling me this? No that was a mentor. Till then I hadn't realized how network marketing success depended hugely on right mentorship. I had always thought it was about 'convincing people' to buy products and enroll. At the coffee shop I was beginning to understand that the only one who needed to be convinced about success was the one I saw in the mirror. This entire industry primarily facilitated that process.

As the attendant returned to clear the mess I'd created with the tea, Nama commented, "you know, to do any business one needs 5 things... Products, Marketing Strategy, Training, Finance and People."

"Right", I said, wondering what that was leading to.

"Let us look at each of these in the context of Network Marketing" he continued. "The product for network marketers is wide open. Anything can flow in the network.

For example, in a telecom network, once your cables are laid, you can flow data, voice, video, text... whatever, through them. Similarly, a network marketer is actually in the business of laying the cables... comprised of consumers consuming good quality products."

"So what you're saying is, as B-quadrant business owners our focus is to maintain the robustness of the cable... the product per se, is immaterial?" I was surprised. Most people I knew earlier started and finished the conversation with the name of the product company.

"Yes, that's what I'm saying. As a network marketer you can be sure you will always have a great product... or in fact various product lines... which is why it is the least of our worries. What's more important is the strategy for success in network marketing. And that's designed to reduce individual work and increase System and team work. By allowing a System to work, every Network Marketer can leverage more from the team than by charting their own strategies."

This I understood. Robert Kiyosaki recommended Network Marketing so passionately because the marketing strategy was set in place by a System. True network marketers will search for a system for success and abide by it... and in doing so would change their everything... from mindset to finances to relationships!

Encouraged by my emphatic nods Nama continued, "Further, in Network Marketing you get training and operating advice for free, from extremely successful business owners! Because they have a vested interest in your success. Every action of yours... the cost-benefit... the effectiveness... the impact... is well known in advance and you can follow footsteps to operate like the best."

"Thanks Nama. You are leading by example. How I wish people would just accept help rather than fight their individual battles with life. This I believe is the most undervalued bonus of Network Marketing… it builds the mindset for leadership in all walks of life. And once that develops everything else is a cakewalk!"

"Hey I'm glad you're discovering! But you know, we have one really interesting difference from conventional business," Nama added teasingly. "For any business to provide larger turnover and profit, the costs of operation increase. Right?" "Right." "Not so in Network Marketing. Here, though the business expands exponentially, the expenses remain at the same level. And they're quite nominal and risk-free."

Now that was so true. As he spoke I realized this is the only business where one could be absolutely in control of cash-flow planning and growth. Which is a severe stress-point in any other business.

"However, since network marketing is a B-quadrant business, the money comes in much after the work is done. It's like in farming, where you plant the seeds in one season and harvest the next season. This ruffles up a lot of people who are used to money-for-effort like in a job or sales. And this is why one must be open to training, to develop the mindset of the rich!"

Coming from a cost accountant, that was an acute financial observation I thought. Probably that's what keeps people away. They want money upfront. That doesn't come. So they don't value training. So their money consciousness doesn't grow. And a vicious downward spiral starts.

"And finally about people. Again, here conventional business and Network Marketing differ significantly. In a traditional business you 'pay' people to follow instructions. In Network Marketing you 'inspire' people to do that. You learn how to lead an army of volunteers. That's what Mandela, Gandhi, Columbus and others set out to do in their lives and look where it got them."

Whew! I felt a bolt of clarity had hit me. You yourself do what needs to be done and teach others how to duplicate the simplicity of that. This is why network marketers are basically in search of open-minded students. Just like the Rotary Club is in search of socially inclined business-persons and the Art-of-Living Community is in search of people willing to be navigated to a higher consciousness. Exciting!

It all seemed to be building up to a final question that was tearing my brains away. "So Nama if network marketing is such a powerful instrument for radical social change, why don't people embrace it more willingly?" As soon as I finished, I wished I hadn't asked. I feared he might say, 'think of your own story'. I was instantly guilty. Fear and guilt. I was operating from the lowest vibrations. But he was vibrating really well. Like a true coach. And so he said nothing. We'd paid for the damages. He just smiled and walked away. My karma was to discover this part myself.

Cut to the beginning

Srinivas Rao was a smart young branch head at an MNC in Hyderabad. I had met him briefly in Mumbai at a Retail Summit. As a consultant I had to be there. As a vendor, he did. The second time I met him was in my office. He called and offered to have the Managing Director of a fast-growing retail store-chain drop by. Some business ideas to toss around. That was not unusual.

"Tomorrow noon?"… "Sure"… "Done!"

Mahesh Raju stepped into all 800 square feet of my proud little office. He was wearing a silly smile. "Hi"… "Hi"… "Hi Srinivas!" Srinivas nodded.

Mahesh spoke as we settled down. We chatted about this and that. The economy. Entrepreneurship. Control and choices. Srinivas did not speak. Even if I would ask Srinivas a direct question he would deflect it to Mahesh. I felt Srinivas was dumber than he first appeared to be.

I later realized that he was really smart. This is a very important lesson for network marketers. When your upline is speaking, you have only one job. Shut up. This way you will not be the 'expert'. And importantly, you will subtly transfer trust and edification to the stranger. Mahesh, in our case, was gaining a trust I would grow to value for life.

Before long Mahesh drew some circles. Spoke about networking. Mentioned Robert Kiyosaki. B-quadrant…

"Yayayaya… I know." That's all I said in summation.

Two years later I read somewhere the wise old saying, "you stop growing the moment you let four words take a place in your mind… and those words are 'I already know that'." It's true. I had not been growing personally or professionally through the preceding 3 and succeeding 2 years of this eventless meeting.

In fact, about 20 minutes into the dialog Mahesh figuratively bowed his hat. "Thanks Sandeep, it was a pleasure to know you."

I already knew that too. My ego beamed benevolently, "Hey Mahesh, the pleasure is mutual. Thanks guys for coming."

A couple of days later Srinivas called to ask if I had a chance to hear any of the tapes he'd left behind. Haughtily I replied, "come on Srini, I'm a brand consultant with 15 years of advertising behind me. My guys write the stuff these tapes have on them."

And that was true. We did have an MLM client and we did understand the people-get-people model very well. We also did understand the value of 'motivating the lesser beings' and developed various materials – CDs, booklets, visual aids, websites – to look slick and 'convince' people. 'What all people will do just to make money' we used to think.

I couldn't help wonder why Mahesh would do something like that. Maybe he's winding up his 3 stores. 'He's in a competitive space'. I had no idea that he had already learned not to look at competitive spaces. That he was well into practicing abundance. He was a B-quadrant operator and I would realize its significance only when he'd set up 16 showrooms and developed a flourishing networking business.

It took about two years for Mahesh to grow from 3 to 16 showrooms. It took me one and a half years to start to read Cashflow Quadrant by Robert Kiyosaki. I didn't read it because Mahesh had told me it would change my life. I read it because another friend casually mentioned that it was a good read.

This is how we are. We will trust the word of a known devil but not of an unknown angel. And this is the trick to network marketing. Become a known devil first. And then keep your words casual. Don't be persuasive, over-excited, salesy, or incredible (it will change your life). Just casual.

Cashflow Quadrant did change my life.

Meanwhile, there was another known devil, Ashok, who had started sending mails all over the Rotary circuit. I had been President of my club and was therefore on many mailing lists. Ashok's messages were arousing curiosity but stank of MLM. Maybe my nose was extra sensitive to messaging as I had been a copywriter early in my career. But Ashok was persuasive. And even after he confirmed it was about network marketing, he made sure we attended a meeting. A BBS. My wife and I did go, only to get ideas for meetings for our own MLM client. But that was one right thing Ashok did. Here's the decisive mail that got us into a meeting environment:

*****

Dear Sandeep,

There is one and only one reason why Donald Trump, Bill Gates, Warren Buffet and Robert Kiyosaki recommend network marketing. And that is the mindset that you develop to leverage people and resources... which is exactly what they do... which is exactly the formula to create wealth.

They believe the world needs more wealth creators. Good employees, for all they are good for, are money suckers from an organization's system. A liability. Marketers - at most - would be assets, if they bring enough money in. But network marketers on the other hand, are assets for their own organizations as well for the system/s they subscribe to.

I find this point is rarely understood by people. Even those people who have been open minded enough to opt in to the network marketing circuit. And I believe that if network marketers are to design the futures of their families with some level of predictability, this is the key point to understand.

Therefore I say it again, phrased differently. If you want to control your success, you need to accept that your traditional knowledge and education is not going to get you there. You need B-quadrant thinking (ref: Robert Kiyosaki) and a good understanding of what actions will put money into your pocket (assets) and what will take it out (liabilities).

Chances are, you still didn't get it (it took me several years to get it myself :-)). And that is the point of this mail. You need a different education, for a different mindset, for success in network marketing. And that education, like any traditional education would require you to go somewhere. Meetings are like the 'schools' for network marketers.

You learn faster if you attend more meetings because your mind develops that much more. It is important at a meeting to not judge or like/dislike. Because you don't really understand what the meeting is doing to your mind anyway. All you have to like is 'the reason why' you will opt for network marketing. Just as you may not have liked Chemistry at school, but liked the idea of becoming a graduate... so you went through the Chem classes, right?

There's no rocket science to this. Just be at the meeting with your wife.

Love, Ashok

*****

That was it. We went. We saw. We came back. We didn't entertain much further discussion. But I didn't realize then, that the 2 hours we spent even as rank outsiders had left an impression on us. Which would return to us later.

Srinivas also did a lot of right things. The way he made contact. The way he shut up. Left material and casually touched back. He was perceptive about my big fat ego which he never mentioned. Maybe if he'd not met in my office, but at home instead, he'd have involved my wife and we'd have sorted matters between us… and who knows, she might have understood the beauty of network marketing earlier and forever. It's always a good idea to share the plan with a couple. It's not a business plan. It's a life plan. A 4-hour work week is not a business. It's life.

So how did Mr. know-it-all Sandeep Nath finally come around? God is kind. Mahesh and I shared the gym at the Jubilee Hills Club. It was always just a courtesy exchange between us. One of my clients was a competitor of his company. And this guy was driving us all nuts before the festive season. Sale offers. Promotions. Merchandise. Discount programs. The consumer electronics industry always went berserk at festivals. But Mahesh was cool. Never missed a beat every morning at the gym. A picture of calm. And the grapevine was abuzz with news of 8 new showrooms he was opening that month.

So one day I gathered the courage to ask, "Hi Mahesh, how's business?"

"Fantastic!"

"Doesn't the expansion and festive shopping keep you busy with inventories and marketing brainstorms?"

"We have systems in place Sandeep."

There was silence. "How did you do it Mahesh?"

"Remember the principles we build our networks on Sandeep? They apply. It's life in the B-quadrant." He smiled and reached for his towel.

Now that was the time I'd just finished reading Cashflow Quadrant. The penny dropped. Impulsively, as though it might be too late if he'd walked away with the towel in hand, I blurted, "Will you teach me?" And before my ego could cover up the earnest desire of an ambitious heart, Mahesh sealed it, "Sure! Shall we meet early evening or around 8 pm?"

Many huge lessons. Always respond affirmative. Always give a choice between 2 yes-answers (never ask a question that can be answered by a yes or a no). Always ask questions to keep control over the conversation. Always practice silence. Don't speak unless spoken to. Become magnetic.

"About 5 pm, my office?"

"Perfect." Another lesson. Everything is perfect. Always. Everything in life is pre-ordained. All you do is keep walking. Be a 'karm yogi' (a doer) as the Gita preaches.

I signed up to learn the system mindset. To 'not be' the expert. To (maybe) make some extra money too. But my wife wasn't prioritizing any of this. She was clouded by our past experiences and our own client. She knew we painted rosy pictures and deluded 'weaker people'. So when Mahesh said we ought to accompany the team for a large seminar in Bangalore, an overnight drive, we declined. We'd already signed up. Thanks to Ashok we knew what a 'big' meeting looked like. Now we weren't going to exert. Let it be clear. "Ya Mahesh, I know. It will be exciting, motivating. I'm already motivated… come back and you'll see."

And so my business stayed dormant for the next several months. Mahesh would keep the team together at Sunday meetings and invite me. One day I relented and showed up. Only because he seemed sincere. And the other guys involved were quite ok too. In fact that's the part that took me by surprise at Ashok's BBS. "These guys are well to do professionals... not the kind we have with our MLM client", I remembered telling my wife. But she had formed a different impression. Of negative coercion. She had not read Ashok's mail. She had not read Kiyosaki. To her the meetings were an intrusion. And to me they became a conduit to a world of positivity and cheer. Before I knew it, networking was in my bloodstream. I had started dreaming again. My life was sorted. Except with her.

*****

While I started my journey from the left quadrants to the B-quadrant she prided herself in becoming the expert. She made more money per hour than I did in a month of networking. Even after Malaysia. But I had by then heard many tapes. I could relate to the stories of successful people with diverse circumstances. I understood the B-quadrant caveat of delayed gratification. I could leverage the system. My aim had become to merge both worlds. Put consulting into a system.

And so I shared the network marketing plan with my clients. My multi-millionaire mentors like Jim and Basil had drilled into me, 'build your organization with people who are peer and above, else you will feel stunted'. It made sense... the Russian doll principle... work with people bigger and better than you and you will grow. Over time I found every principle I learned here facilitated excellence in my profession. I and wished it for my clients too...

I picked up the phone and spoke with the first one.

"Mr. Ramesh, hello! I have an idea for you to diversify. We can talk about it over tea at Vikas's place (his son and heir to their business empire). Would you prefer today evening or tomorrow?" "Tomorrow." "Done. About 6 pm or would you prefer 8?" "8 might be better." "Great! I'll see you both. Thanks." Click. Always invite on phone… never in person.

"Ahmed bhai, good afternoon! How's everything?" "Sandeep?" "Yes! It's been quite a while but I've been thinking of you." "Really! Why?" "I met a lady called Tharini Nama recently and she's a health consultant. In fact she's an expert on weight management. And I thought of your wife… what's her name?" "Afsha?" "Yes Afsha! How's she doing? Is she still bothered by the weight problem as she was when we last met?" "Maybe, we haven't discussed that lately." "Right Ahmed bhai, you'll probably be busy and I don't want to bother you. I am trying to get Tharini's time. Could I have Afsha's number and perhaps the two of them could fix up a suitable time to talk it over?" "Ok, I guess … here's the number"…

"Hello is that Afsha?" "Yes" "Hi Afsha, this is Sandeep Nath. I had met you and Ahmed bhai at the hitex exhibition, you remember? Ahmed is a client of ours." "Hmmm…" "That's ok Afsha, you will perhaps remember when we meet. I called to check if you would still be looking for solutions for the weight issue you seemed very troubled by, back then." "Maybe…" "Well great! I recently came across a certain Mrs. Tharini Nama who is doing magic with weight loss. Would you like to meet up with me so I can give you a background about it?" "Let me check with Ahmed…" "Great! I just spoke with him. In fact he gave me your number. Tell me when you're free at home and I'll check if Mrs. Nama is available too. How's

Thursday evening for you?" "Oh on Thursday we have a wedding." "Friday then?" "Maybe." "Great, I'll reconfirm and can we keep a spot open for Saturday afternoon also... just in case?" "Ok."

Now she'd make sure Ahmed would be with her on Friday and I'd show the plan. And Saturday would be clear for the follow-up and Tharini as well.

And this way, life went on. Many 'nos', some 'yeses'. And some great lessons for life.

The path to success winds its way through failure. This is contrary to popular thought. We are taught that 'pass' is the opposite of 'fail'. Which assumes that we are in the middle of the two. Either we pass an exam or we fail it. But in life, we are actually at one end of the spectrum, failure is in the centre and pass is at the other end, beyond failure. Our road to success is thus paved with failures. And it is only when we study extraordinary lives that the truth of this stares in the face. This is not a truth for a mediocre life. A mediocre life is not affected by this spectrum in real terms at all. And that's why mediocre is ordinary whereas these people were extraordinary...

- *Lucille Ball worked as a hat girl and waitress for 22 years before she landed her first major acting role*
- *Retired Colonel Harlan Sanders gave samples to 1009 restaurants before selling his chicken recipe... popular today as* KFC
- *Alex Haley spent 12 years and was $100,000 in debt when he found a publisher for his book,* Roots

- *Winston Churchill's school reports often stated, "no ambition, poor academic work and disruptive behavior"*

- *Walt Disney was told by a Kansas City news editor that his sketches showed no talent. He was rejected many times over.*

- *Thomas Edison tried over 10,000 times to invent the light-bulb before he met success, laying the foundation for GE*

- *Albert Einstein was four years old before he could speak… one of his teachers stated, "he'll never amount to anything"*

The lesson is to 'go' for 'no'. In network marketing, however bad one might be, after 20 'nos' one will find a 'yes'. That's the law of averages. The numbers game.

So (I recalled from the day I cracked LC) if it took 50 yeses to go diamond, that would be 1000 nos. "How soon can I collect 1000 nos?" was the question I was asking myself. That was the only physical planning required. The rest was mental planning. About what these 'nos' would do to my mind. Dealing with that, I learned, was what made professional networkers great. Mahesh once forwarded this story to me for context…

*****

During the great depression, Alina, a young girl, was torn apart. She had lost her child, had a jobless husband, influenza in the neighborhood, a cracked roof overhead (through which the dripping rain was no pleasure). It was not easy. The only person she felt she could speak with was her mum, a wise young lady of 45, who was herself in no better shape, even though she was 5 hours away in the countryside.

Alina decided she would go see her mum. Somehow that lady had borne the burden of war and they both remembered those days vividly. "Mum will have a message for me", Alina thought.

It was an arduous journey to say the least. The highways you see today were obviously non-existent. But she got home somehow and doused herself in the comfort of her mother's warmth. Brave for a fleeting moment... and awash with tears the very next. Mum understood. That's why she's a mum, right?

She guided Alina to the kitchen and filled 3 pots with water and placed them on the fire. Without a word spoken, she placed a couple of carrots in one; and egg in the other; and some coffee beans in the third. In a few minutes all three came to boil. She removed them one by one.

Now mum turned to Alina and said, "darling, feel the carrots and tell me how they are."

"Soft and shapeless", Alina said.

"And the egg? Break it and see." Alina did as she was told and found the egg was hard on the inside now.

"What about this?" mum asked, pouring the pot of coffee into a mug and it handing it over for Alina to drink. "Mum this is soooo fantastic", Alina exclaimed, her eyes lighting up for once!

"Yes dear, it is, isn't it?" Drawing a deep breath mum continued, "this is life Alina. And adversity is a part of it. Here you saw all three subject to the same adversity... the boiling water... and the carrot went in tough and proud but couldn't stand up to it. The egg went in with an innocent, pliable heart but the circumstances caused it to

harden up. It now holds grossness that will stay with it for life, though no one would be able to tell the difference from outside."

"And the coffee beans mum?"

"And it was the beans darling that took upon themselves to 'go over' the circumstances. They made sure that after the testing times were through, the times became better for everyone."

*****

Now this is what professional networkers do. Become coffee beans. Change the state of their surroundings and make a difference in this world.

Surely we might not start off as coffee beans but anyone can learn to be them. Just like we learn karate. Arjun, a black belt, taught me two important principles about it.

One, that we need to toughen our hands by hitting hot sand. Success (strong hands) lies beyond failure (ouch! hot sand). Network marketing does for the mind what karate does for the hand. Makes it strong. Gives it resilience.

With each 'no' I was experiencing my mental arms toughening up. Because my issue was, which part did I want to earn my money from? My mind or my body? So what was I feeding? Exercising? Strengthening?

Second, Arjun said, if we have to slice through a pile of bricks, even as a karate black belt we might break our hand if we focused on the bricks. The trick was to focus beyond the bricks. That's how we would slice through them before we lost the energy of impact.

Likewise, to succeed in network marketing we must focus on a goal far beyond the obvious benefits. Which is why the invitation to view the project is never about the money, products or opportunity. It is casual. And aimed at opening the mind to 'possibility thinking'. And of course it takes a lot of practice and failing to get this right! But once the mind knows what it wants, achieving it is really a cake walk. And the impact is life-changing for life.

Author's note:

Getting the invitation right is the crux of building a network marketing business. You must be professional about it and understand that it is your business you are inviting people to partner with. It's not your upline's business or the manufacturer's business. It's got your name and your family's dream written all over it. Treat it with respect as you talk about it with others. Talk with integrity after having personally used the products. Learn the right way to invite and write your ticket to success.

Will we always be like this?

'We' have evolved as a human race but we often forget that the prehistoric years continue to have a profound bearing on our psyche. We were in the stone ages for 200,000 years and came to some form of civilization only about 8,000 years ago. To expect our thinking to have changed since 'civilization' dawned is like expecting a 100 year old man to change and behave like a 4 year old just because they spent 4 years together. The old man had lived 96 years even before the kid came on the scene. Likewise mankind had lived 192,000 years before the civilized mind even entered. Obviously mankind's thought patterns would be deep-set.

Our consciousness rests upon the early foundation years, when hunting was a way of life, barter was the exchange and gender roles were well defined (John Gray makes a great point about this in his book, 'Men are from Mars; Women are from Venus'). Anything we do to work against this collective consciousness we falter with. It's that simple.

We bungle up relationships. We have trouble with career women. We don't know whether currency is good or bad. We are confused.

******

"It is time for central banks to stop pretending that zero is the floor for nominal interest rates. There is no theoretical or practical reason for not having the Federal Funds target rate and market rates at, say, minus five percent, if that is what your Taylor rule, or whatever heuristic guides your official policy rate, suggests.

Economics as a science and economic reality have never had problems with negative real (inflation-adjusted) interest rates. So what is the problem with nominal rates? In a word, it's currency.

Currency is the only problem. Paying positive interest on currency is difficult because you don't know the identity of the owner. The same note could be presented repeatedly to earn the interest due for a single period. To get around this problem, the instrument itself must be clearly identified as current or non-current on interest. Once interest has been paid, it is marked, traditionally by stamping it or by clipping a coupon off it.

With negative interest, the problem is not the owner turning up too often to claim his interest. It is getting him to turn up at all. Since the authorities don't know I am the owner of the currency I own, why should I volunteer to pay the government money for the privilege?

Fortunately, it turns out to be extremely simple to remove the zero lower bound on short, risk-free nominal interest rates. There are three practical ways to implement negative nominal interest rates.

(1) Abolish currency.

(2) Tax currency and 'stamp' it to show it is 'current on interest due'.

(3) Unbundle currency from the unit of account."

*****

Quoting Thomas Jefferson (1810 – two centuries before the above report!)

"That we are overdone with banking institutions which have banished the precious metals and substituted a more fluctuating and unsafe medium, that these have withdrawn capital from useful improvements and employments to nourish idleness, that the wars of the world have swollen our commerce beyond the wholesome limits of exchanging our own productions for our own wants, and that, for the emolument of a small proportion of our society who prefer these demoralizing pursuits to labors useful to the whole, the peace of the whole is endangered and all our present difficulties produced, are evils more easily to be deplored than remedied."

*****

Quoting Robert Hemphill, US Federal Judge (circa 1970)

"If all the bank loans were paid, no one could have a bank deposit, and there would not be a dollar of coin or currency in circulation. This is a staggering thought. We are completely dependent on the commercial Banks. Someone has to borrow every dollar we have in circulation, cash or credit. If the Banks create ample synthetic money we are prosperous; if not, we starve. We are absolutely without a permanent money system. When one gets a complete grasp of the picture, the tragic absurdity of our hopeless position is almost incredible, but there it is. It is the most important subject intelligent persons can investigate and reflect upon. It is so important that our present civilization may collapse unless it becomes widely understood and the defects remedied very soon."

******

What this means is, unless majority of us stay in debt there will be no money to circulate in the economy and currency exchange will come to a grinding halt resulting in another great depression. What a negative cycle of consciousness that is! And why do we subscribe to it?

Robert Kiyosaki calls it the conspiracy of the rich. And then he goes on to tell us how network marketing is the great leveler. The opportunity for each individual family to develop and thrive in their own economy. It's distributed wealth. Like distributed power. Many households in Europe generate solar power in surplus on their rooftops. And they feed the surplus to the grid and make money from it. Many households in India construct an extra room and toilet to let out as paying-guest accommodation for extra cash. What are these? Backyard assets. Micro-economies. Functioning for individual benefit within the economic superspace.

Network marketing is just that sort of trend. You create a network of like minded consumers. Since you use products that you buy directly from the manufacturer, the manufacturer saves money on the wholesaler-retailer-advertising supply chain. He would rather pass it over to a 'loyal' consumer group. But how would he create loyalty? He'd incentivize leaders who would manage a loyal network for him. Pay everyone who consumes across the board and pay more to people who don the B-quadrant leadership role. That's all.

The potential for asset creation in network marketing is boundless. People buy private jet planes with the money lying on the table. Of course, it's because they're visionaries. And they've mastered the B-quadrant principles. Do you want a private jet? If yes, perhaps you don't have many other strategies to get it, do you? And this is one where you'll get it through a systematic step-by-step process.

Are all network marketing companies the same? No. There are many different network building strategies. There are many different product lines. From telephones to vitamins to novelty items to education and household goods… the list is large. What's common everywhere is that the consumer is directly connected to the source and therefore enjoys a money back guarantee (often even after she's opened the product seal and used the product). She also enjoys home delivery with most large network marketing companies. And of course the support of a team that would teach her how to 'think' to make full use of the new economic model.

In fact, this support and teaching by fellow-entrepreneurs, as Nama had pointed out at the coffee shop, is quite alien in the corporate world. Given the competitive spirit (characteristic of the left quadrants), it is rare to see people helping each other succeed. In the consciousness we operate from in a job situation, 'trust' has a low standing. In fact it is considered foolish to shut one's brains off and trust another. People are actually paid to investigate other's affairs. 'Due diligence' it is euphemistically called.

Of course, many new network marketers have indeed burned their fingers by trusting other newbies who were also operating from a low vibration. But I believe this mustn't prevent anyone from hooking up with the right community when one finds it. The loss, if any, due to associating with an untrustworthy individual or company will be far less than the potential gain of creating your own backyard assets.

One would ideally attach as much significance to a misplaced choice of networking company or upline as one would to a bad car mechanic… a poor experience with him wouldn't deter one from driving, would it?

This was the essence of a team discussion at Nama's place the next Sunday morning. It fascinated me. I had been into some part of my spiritual journey and I found it fascinating how a simple concept like this tied in with a huge mindset shift into the realm of abundance. That was the first time I opened my mouth that morning. "Nama, are you saying that being in the company of professional network builders will bring about an abundance mentality in us?"

"Wow! That's a great conclusion... how did you arrive at that?"

"Well I'm just trying to put the pieces together I guess", I said, examining my nails for I really had no clue what I was talking about.

Sonia was kind to interject, "Abundance is a natural state of mind. I am sure the stone-age man lived in abundance of everything he needed. Air, water, food, caves... it's education that curbs it..." Ravi cut in, "but Sonia he also lived in fear."

"Right!" I found myself saying, "and all of technology has evolved only to conquer fear. Everything mankind has initiated has been so that we would not have to live in the lower vibrations of fear, guilt and shame."

"For example?"

"Well dynamite and atom bombs came about so we could survive... we have no shame in killing others, as long as we ourselves escape death", I declared. "Even with the stone-age man, let's take the wheel... it came about because it could move us faster than predatory animals. So we have been addressing our fears since then. And recently, the internet and sms became popular so we could escape the guilt of not being in touch with each other… think about it… conquering lower vibration is the incentive for anything to have been invented."

Mahesh laughed. "I remember seeing 'The Gods Must Be Crazy' some years back. We've really screwed up our lives. All our education teaches us how to cope with the technology we've invented. Takes us really far from nature and our natural abundant selves. Better fear one elephant than a hundred clients!"

Sonia was not sure though she couldn't stop giggling. Nama decided this was getting out of hand. "Hey guys that's not the point really, is it? Sandeep mentioned 'abundance' and there are three things we must know about it. Shall we begin?" We again listened attentively.

"One is a concept of the nature of money. Unless we tune our minds to think differently about money we are not going to have the holistic lives people in the B-quadrant lead. What you must do is drop your hang-up about my-money, your-money. Money is like water. There is plenty. Like if you visualize a river. It is in motion. You can tap what you like from it. Once you use some you forget about it and get fresh water for the next use. You can even canalize it for some productive use. Are you with me?" "Yes." "Yes." "Pretty much." "Cool."

"Now what you are learning as you practice network marketing is how to lay a pipeline of money from the money river to your home. It's pretty different from your job or business where you get a bucketful home every month, or with every project you do. The money river is the consumer economy and when you think a bucket is all you have, you restrict your abundance. But when you can clearly visualize the pipeline and work diligently towards building it, you are into abundance."

"Voila! So this pipeline is the consumer network, right? And it can have many tributaries," Sunil exclaimed in a eureka voice.

"Exactly! That's the help you give to people."

"And create prosperity from the river of abundance."

"But I want the whole river," cut in Mahesh abruptly. "Huh??" we went.

Nama picked up a cookie and slurped on his now-empty glass of juice, slowly, carefully measuring each of the 3 words he uttered, "Become the sea."

Become the sea. Profound. Become the sea. The thought would stay with me till I lived. You don't 'just get' what you want. You 'become' what you want. Mahatma Gandhi 'became' the revolutionary in order to create the army of peaceful revolutionaries he envisioned. George Washington became the warrior when his only option was to have lay-peasants take up arms. Mother Teresa became the messiah to have the largest fraternity of messiahs in the world. Princess Diana became the queen of hearts to be remembered as more of a queen than The Queen herself. Become the sea... and thou shalt have all the rivers.

Somehow the discussion ended that day without us getting to the other two points. The juices got over. Glasses clinked. The team felt great... ready to face another week of bogus negativity – at the store, in the school, with the boss, around the in-laws... Team meetings were like the oasis. And Sunday to Sunday, life was progressive.

Having finished with showing the plan to a half-dozen or so new prospects, we got them packing with some CDs and were on the floor again next Sunday. "Abundance Nama, three things..." Sonia was not one to forget quickly.

"Yep", Nama smiled, "actually I'd like Tharini to speak about the second one as she's the one who juggles the household finances." As the beaming Tharini got up to speak, I couldn't help but miss my wife. If only she understood... it's such fun as a couple.

Tharini began, "Well I don't know much about other networks but as network builders in the consumer products space, we focus mainly on our own consumption of products. We're not driven by selling. We're driven by being role models. Product ambassadors, who can use the products, benefit from them, and then speak with integrity when we share with others the opportunity to benefit as prosumers."

"Prosumers?" That was Vivek in a sing-song voice. He was just a couple of days old and was a quick willing learner... therefore at the smaller Sunday session.

"Yes, prosumer as in profit-sharing-consumer. Also since pro is the opposite of con, as a prosumer you don't get conned." We all laughed. Vivek didn't get the joke. Tharini was sensitive about it and explained, "Whatever you buy from the market has a margin for the retailer, the wholesaler and the celebrity who endorses it, right? " "Right." "So whatever price you might buy an item at, you are still paying for someone else's Mercedes right?" "Hmmm." "You may think you are saving money buying 2 for the price of 1, but actually the product costs one third and except for during the sale, you are paying two-thirds extra… by habit… without conscious thought."

Vivek checked, "And now we're saying I can change my buying habits and buy products direct from manufacturer, right?" "Absolutely right." "But the products are expensive!"

"Exactly! And that's where your consciousness as a prosumer gets built. You see network marketing products are typically designed and patented as concentrated formulations. This helps save on inventory, stocking and transport costs, so the savings can be shared with prosumers. Now as a prosumer you must internalize two things. One, that concentrates will cost more than the glitzy looking well stocked products on the market shelves. And second, because your products will call for an upfront expense they will help you budget better and bring you in heightened consciousness of money."

I had experienced this step-up of money consciousness first-hand. It had taken me 3 months to get over the idea of spending `600 on a detergent. But when I finally did, and the blessed product lasted 4 months, I was happy to never again put the 'cheaper' `150 detergent on my monthly grocery list. Consequently, when I could visualize a `600 detergent, and derive value from it, I had stretched my mind four times to visualize a `1,200,000 car as well. And that shift in consciousness actually put us in that car, which was a big move from the earlier one which we'd bought at one-fourth the cost. Another step forward on the ladder of abundance!

"Money consciousness is a mind game. Have you all read 'Secrets of the Millionaire Mind' by Harv Eker?" Most of us nodded. Read it if you haven't, and practice this game on yourself. Tharini went on to tell us the game which proved to be extremely helpful for all of us to remodel our money consciousness for free! (see appendix 3)

"So what you're saying Tharini, is our money consciousness increases as we mentally tune our expenses at a higher level… is that right?" I asked.

"Right. And with network marketing products, since we have the model built in favor of the prosumer, we expand our money consciousness without really draining our pockets. Plus the money flows back as share of profit."

"I have still to see that" said Vivek.

"You will certainly," piped in Nama, "all you need to do is trust your team and follow instructions step by step. They've walked the road. They're making the money. You hang in close to them and do what they do. Makes sense?"

"Sure does… a no-brainer actually."

"But", and this was characteristically me, "But Nama, why do so few people actually do that?"

"It's fear motivation at work Sandeep. They hear someone say something negative or derogatory and fear that they are being misled. It doesn't matter how misinformed their informer might be. The society at large fears what other people think. And the sad fact is, nobody actually thinks. When was the last time you 'thought' about what a close friend does for a living? Possibly never." Hmmm. Nama had a point. "But this brings me to the third aspect of abundance thinking" continued Nama, "and that's about the feeling abundance invokes in us."

"I think I can tell" sprang up Sonia, forever springy in word and action. "Abundance invokes the feeling of peace."

"Bingo! How did you arrive at that?"

"Spiritual experience." Sonia had been involved with some great spiritual masters from South India who rendered discourses that attuned the mind into thinking abundance. Initially these programs didn't attract me. Since these courses were for many days on end and I didn't have that kind of time. Moreover there was nothing practical one could do to measure one's progress and yet it required an hour of daily meditation. I'd rather spend my hour listening to multi-millionaires on CDs I'd decided. And both were good choices… devastatingly good as a combination I later learned when I got into the time-abundance mindset and started meditating as well.

Sonia had already discovered the combination and that was why she was manifesting abundance as a contented achiever. The top network marketers are really cool. Coooool. Nothing and nobody can be abrasive to them. It's an inner peace that radiates. It's like a magnetic alignment they have inside and that comes through association. Basil was like that whenever I saw him. Calm. Unfazed. And he too was like an ordinary piece of iron some years back. With the right association he became 'magnetic' and as a life mission, he's helping 'align' ordinary iron pieces like Sonia and me.

This is a self-realization one is not likely to have in an employee environment. Only the business owners have it and that's why most of them seem pious. Piety and alignment have a deep connection with fostering inner peace. Peace is the highest vibration. A handful of peaceful people can change the world as Dr. David Hawkins has propounded. And Gandhi has demonstrated.

*****

When this book falls into your hands… when you read it… what you focus on as you read… it is all predefined by your karma. If your timing is set out to be an early adopter of the new economy – a friend of the trend – this could be your trigger. You would take small steps. Maybe check me out online at SandeepNath.com and look up my associations. I can't say. Maybe you'd just rubbish it the way I did my sister… only to return a few years later.

*****

In 2009 something new happened with me. I decided I would seriously get online and study the internet based economy. I could sense a lot was happening out there and five years down the road I would be a dinosaur if I didn't get cued in. So I took small steps. Meditation – Consulting – Coaching – Networking – And exploring online – all in a single day. "It's like tying your shoelaces", I'd heard Basil say, "everything is difficult before it is easy." Soon I was doing it all as a second nature.

Online I met a community I could not believe existed. The finest peaceful abundance thinkers on the planet. Mike Dillard was one of them. Norbert Orlewicz was another. What I liked was a signature line in his mails, "To your success, Norbert." Why was this complete stranger wishing for my success, I wondered. True, as network marketers we always think of the success of others, but I wasn't even on his network. And that was when it dawned upon me. The internet is the mother of all networks. The place where all the 'rivers' converged. The sea!

Become the sea.

That exchange between Mahesh and Nama suddenly gained new meaning. I could take up all my interests online, I discovered. Share. Network. Write. Coach. Be me. And I set up many sites. One of them was in partnership with a man called Jay Kubassek. This guy struck me as a great leader. He was on a sharply focused mission to create 100 millionaires by 2012. In 4 years I thought. That's $250,000 per person per year. What was he doing? How was he so sure? What was the magic about 2012? Colin Tipping talked of world consciousness crossing the 210 mark by then. Sai Baba visualized grass-root level changes across the Muslim fraternity starting that year. David Hawkins flagged 2012 as a significant year for several reasons. Are these the coincidences James Redfield wanted us to become aware of in The Celestine Prophecy?

Why did Jay articulate my dream with a deadline? I dreamed of coaching and creating 100 B-quadrant business owners in my lifetime. (Needless to say, they'll all be multi-

66

millionaires). Was Jay showing me the path to my dream? Perhaps yes. And since I'd decided to walk in the B-quadrant path he'd laid out online I came across a place where the Robert Kiyosakis, Wayne Allen Roots and the Paul Zane Pilzers of the world hung out. A new leaf was turning.

Anything is possible

It was spring again. As the warmth of the morning sun tickled my feet through the soft blanket, an idea started forming in my mind.

By now I had one major success to speak of... I had cultivated an abundance-thinking mindset, which meant, regardless of the circumstances I could always find myself in a state of plenty. Whether that meant plenty of options, money, goodwill, grace... it was always there. Mentally, in a way, I had moved to the B-quadrant... from being a lone ranger to becoming a connected being. Connected to higher energy.

From being a 'polyclinic' to becoming a 'multi-specialty hospital chain', as a medico would think of it. In fact, medicine and networking did have a lot of parallels, I reflected.

Both had taken centuries in their evolution and both were continuously evolving. Like 'energy medicine' though, networking remained a subject of exploration.

Both supported life, though networking was proactive and medicine reactive.

Medicine was designed to help people physically. Networking was designed to help people financially.

Both operated on the premise of helping others.

Both had a huge drop out rate. While millions applied for medical school, there were just a handful of top medical practitioners in any city. Likewise, while millions were recruited into various networks only a few made it to diamond and above.

Both paid exceedingly well to those who mastered the skills of the trade. Medicine however, still called for active work. Networking paid passive income.

Both also had ramifications and specialties that the majority did not understand. Networkers used less jargon however, and didn't feel offended when people used terms like network distribution and network marketing inter-changeably. (Call a cardio-thoracic surgeon a cardiologist and prepare for a funeral, I was told). Likewise MLMs and private franchises would be as apart as allopathic medicine and homeopathy... but for the world at large these differences did not exist.

Furthermore, both medicine and networking were divinely connected. Their biggest achievements required professional application supported by deep visualization techniques and belief.

And finally, with either, anything was possible.

Anything? Yes!

I once met a gentleman named Doug Wead who was born a church minister's son. He said he didn't have any 'silly dream' of owning a house, a car or even of traveling the world. In spite of that, his sponsor insisted that he dig deep and put a finger on his dream. What would he really want in life? And Doug, being an avid follower of history, concluded, "I want to have a place in history."

As Doug went though the motions of professional networking, days passed. Months passed. And in a few years, he found himself interviewing President Nixon, dining with Ronald Reagan, accompanying Gorbachev on his US tour. He found himself a place in the Whitehouse as special advisor to 2 US Presidents. He was traveling all over the world where history was being written. Berlin. Kazakhstan, Tiananmen. He wrote biographies of great leaders. He loved to write but had only 2 books to his credit before his network marketing days. Since then he wrote 26 more and is counting.

All because the passive income from his network gave him the much needed time. And the resources to publish what he chose to, and meet whoever he wished to!

He developed the contacts. And put the money to use for others. Doug's charitable organization funds the Missionaries of Charity (Mother Teresa) in Kolkata. His resources support scores of AIDS affected villages in Africa. His trucks were the first to reach Tsunami victims in Indonesia. Doug is in history. And that was his dream!

Another gentlemen I came across was the former Vice President of Citibank in Indonesia. Robert Ankasa; a man who dreamed of being a top gun in his industry and a role model.

An ordinary middle class student, he cleaned toilets in Australia to finance his post-graduate management studies... but he says, that's what taught him "to become a guy who could focus on the ends and not be stuck on the means." That was the real education which helped him switch from management at the bank to leadership of his network. And before he was 30 he was hailed as a visionary and inspiration for many middle class Indonesians and people the world over.

Ankasa – through his network marketing opportunity – personally mentored over 50 families to diamond and above. His asset base would be worth several hundred million dollars. And it all developed over a decade, of which three years he spent building a network in parallel to his high pressure bank job. After which he was free. For life. Forever. To serve as an instrument of substantial socio-economic change in Indonesia and – by example – in the rest of the world.

Jim Dornan made a special mention of Ankasa in his path-breaking book co-authored with the legendary John Maxwell, 'Becoming a person of influence'. In a lighter vein he'd said, "it is not falling into a lake that will drown you... it is staying there that will." What he meant was, 'it is not the fact that we are born in a poor environment that makes us miserable. It is our choice to stay in that environment that does that'.

So as we plunge into unknown waters, it is best to keep moving. Else we drown and that's the end of our story in this life. Likewise in the unknown waters of network marketing. Unless we do the work (of guiding people), we would just be another failure statistic. And we'd lose the opportunity to really live our dreams.

*****

I called Nama, hurling the blanket to a side as I was actually feeling quite hot. Was it the heat of my idea? Oh God… why does the phone ring longest when you want it picked fast?

"Morning boss… I have an idea… I want to structure the network marketing industry and build a specialized school to train people in higher consciousness."

One could always share ones dreams with Nama. With any upline for that matter. Dreams are safe with uplines. And they are reinforced by teamwork. If your uplines know exactly what you want, they will help you get it. Because they know the universal law, 'if you can help enough people get what they want, you will get what you want,'

"Splendid", Nama replied encouragingly, "what do you mean by structuring the industry?"

"Well, you know, I can think of multilevel marketing, network marketing, network distribution and private franchising as the four major ramifications of network building. I want to develop distributed centers that are like super-specialty hubs where networkers and other energy-related professionals can come together and create vibrations that impact the world" I gushed.

"Whoa, whoa, whoa, you're going too fast… what are you talking about Sandeep?"

That was one of my bottlenecks he'd hit on. I generally thought faster than I spoke and I spoke faster that others could comprehend and I never figured out whether it was my thoughts they didn't follow or my words. Now thanks to my network mentors I had learned to ask questions… thus sealing the communication gaps that were inevitable earlier.

"Ummm… I think I should just organize my mind and call back. Is there anything you got from what I said so far?

"I can tell you're excited," Nama said, "but do remember Henry Ford's line… you can not build a reputation on what you are going to do."

"Right." That was what I had to hear. This was not the time to talk about it. But this was the time to set out my vision with clarity and work upon widening this holistic network of high consciousness individuals and structuring my financial plan to eke out an institution. "Thanks… will talk later."

And I got back to study the components again. With a pen and paper in hand I began to write the major segments where I'd find the high consciousness people in network building… the diamonds and above attached to…

MLM: They practiced the traditional multi-level marketing model that worked on a multiple tier strategy to enable people on a network to create income through sales of product and the redistribution of commissions thereof.

Network marketing: These people operated on a relatively evolved mechanism of MLM involving various network structuring strategies (not just a binary or matrix model) and modular constructs for leadership development and independent business ownership.

Network distribution: The focus here is not as much on the network structure as on the distribution (as opposed to personal sale) of product. This was a system that any product company could leverage, while network marketing and MLM were systems they would need to own. Network distribution would not necessarily be multi-tiered and could involve redistribution of cash as well.

Private franchising: This combined the empowerment model of independent business owners in network marketing with the systematic cookie-cutter approach of franchising. People in this segment typically got off to a slow start but built solid structures of networks.

Now my idea was that whatever mechanism people might use... whatever product might flow... if they wielded a position of leadership in any such network they would have a high vibration and steady high consciousness. How could we harness that together? I thought I'd take an opinion of a friend outside of all this who had also read Dr. Hawkins' book. His response, right off the bat, stumped me.

"Aren't these pyramids that have people make money off the backs of others?" That was the only thing 'industry structuring' meant to him. And with that starting point I estimated it would be quite a climb to get him to appreciate that the leadership in these organizations vibrate at the highest levels.

"Is that really how you see it Suresh, or are you just echoing some hearsay?" I asked as naturally as I could.

"Well, that's a common perception... I really don't know this industry from inside" he confessed.

"Well," I said, "you've just helped me identify my starting point then. And that is to counter all the ponzis who have made a quick buck from networking through the last century. They have capitalized on the potential of raising hope in the masses. And have let them down miserably."

"Opportunists precede every revolution just as rats precede the flood. It's is a law of nature..." remarked Suresh a little philosophically.

We talked of other things but obviously my mind was elsewhere. To me it was becoming increasingly evident that this industry was not the route. Energy was not the route. Perhaps Kiyosaki was the route. Since I too had entered that way. Could I get business leaders from all over ... people operating B-quadrant enterprises ... to come over and speak at my institute? Let students see the value and the apparent energy and correlate that energy with networkers and move into networking as the foundation themselves?

Or maybe I could call the owners of credible network distribution companies for starters... to maintain cohesiveness. The founder of Amway had served as the Chairman of the US Chambers of Commerce also. We needed people to know that this was mainstream stuff. I thought I'd take this into the next Sunday meeting.

And so I started with a prelude that would get everyone thinking. "The world of network marketing is evolving and booming before our eyes. But that makes it vulnerable. I'd like to use the world of Internet as an example to illustrate my point. Today a technology can come which can wipe out everything that worked yesterday. Google did that when it wept out other search engines... not that Alta Vista was not a good search engine... but well, Google's algorithms were worth billions more. Tomorrow there may be some other. So, it's the same with network marketing... how do you pick a network marketing company that will be safe?"

Characteristically, Nama teed off, "Well, unlike Internet, networking companies with strong roots will always win. How old a company is, is critical. Whatever might be said about technology and methodologies, the saying 'old is gold' is sound. If you have been hearing of the Amway name since 50 years, it is because it's the largest holder of product patents... has the most companies tied up to its distribution network... and is the most respected and awarded direct sales corporation according to United Nations and Governments worldwide."

Quite true Krishna chipped in, "An older organization is 'built to last' as per the principles of any corporate business. Or put another way, the older a network marketing company is, the deeper its pipelines and therefore the more secure your future."

"But an old company is saturated" someone said.

"Saturation! That's a joke. It will be real only when products moving through consumer networks will garner more than 10% share of their respective industries. In 50 years even Amway doesn't have a 1% share in most categories," countered Sai. "And it's close to ten billion dollars in size."

Sonia offered a different perspective. "I'd think the most important thing for a company to be safe is to know who its leaders are. Network marketing works on leverage, so if a company's founding leadership is strong, it will duplicate well. There will be values, integrity and commitment. And adaptability to new circumstances as the need may be…"

The discussion was getting charged now. From across the room Srinivas couldn't contain himself and interjected, "How about how widespread are they? If you are getting into a business of your own, piggybacking on the franchise of a known brand, you may as well pick the brand that is spread all over the world, right?"

Anant took over, "An international company also means it is one that has seen numerous cultures, legalities, psychographics and has prepared itself for success through all of that."

Nand watched from the centre as the discussion ping-ponged around. I had expected him to say "match-point" or some such thing to lighten the discussion and tune it with the Wimbledon mood in the air, but he was actually looking for the space… and he got it. "Well, the good thing about network marketing is cash. It is a cash business - no credit. No debt. No liabilities. And that's the mindset its partners also eventually get into… So you would like to check if this is true of your company. If not, why not? Is it a justifiable loan they've taken? Will the company repay or could they possibly pocket the money and fly away into the night?"

Peeved that he didn't think of that in spite of his being a chartered accountant Anant added, "well, 'how old it is' helps. Plus there are published facts. This is not something you learn by hearsay… you find out from Euromonitor or some large data house."

By now people were generally nodding their heads and wondering if that quick fire had left anything to be said before this subject could be buried. And Lakshmi brought out that there was.

"Without training your business is like a vehicle you don't know how to drive… Just a shiny object in the garage. I have a bias to companies that have product training but also have separate Training and Support Systems set up by successful affiliates of the company. These are good because they are practical. What do you think?"

"Absolutely" I said for I felt that way too. "For example, a guy who works at the Ferrari factory would not be able to teach you how to drive a Ferrari as well as a race car driver would. So the System set up by race car drivers using Ferrari is better than Ferrari's own training. That's why it makes sense to look for a combination of two companies to make the infrastructure work harder for your success!"

Having said that I suddenly noticed that each point being made was a reflection of the individual's own thought process… his or her own justification and reason why they had opted in to this industry. And that would imply, that as more people understood the reasons to pick a stable company, more people would get involved. 'I must remember to publish this on my blog,' I thought, happy to now have an internet presence as well.

Just then Nama piped in, "Before you conclude, allow me to mention that the Product and Compensation plan have not been forgotten. It's just that they are not key. And the reason they really don't matter is because every network marketing company does have products that are good for large numbers of people. And they do price them and distribute the monies in a way that maximum people benefit, whether new or old in their association. So if either of these things do not agree with a prospect, it just indicates that they've either not understood the opportunity or the network marketing model itself."

"Rah rah! What a befitting conclusion" I said, happy to have got a lot of points from this exercise.

Next I moved the discussion to the key challenges before people making the choice for financial freedom, and networking as the means to it.

"Safety apart, do people have the requisite clarity on their dreams? Networking is a common practice in society. But coupling professional networking practices with a dream is what we do here. Generally people well-educated in the left quadrants scoff at the concept of dreams. But dreams are powerful," I asked, sparking the idea.

"Well, Robert Kiyosaki says there are two types of rich, 'the rich who have money and the rich who don't yet have the money. And then there are the poor; who may or may not have money but it is never enough'" quoted Hari. "My guess is network marketing is only for the Kiyosaki rich... they are dreamers."

"Not necessarily Hari. If 'rich' means you do not spend your time to earn money and 'middle class' means you do not abuse your body to earn money, 'poor' would refer to people who earn money using their physical body. And all three would qualify for our industry… whatever their upbringing", challenged Aarti emphatic about including everyone as a prospect, as she got up to refill her glass of juice.

Walking along she continued, "Now there is a lot to be said about this 'upbringing' because it is often the main reason we stay middle class. The root lies in conformity. Do what the neighbors do! What will our friends think? But here's news… hang out with rich friends and conformity will pull you up rather than keep you where you are."

"Right… so the first step is to Decide to Be Rich" said Hari happy to find his point back. "Stop feeling sorry for yourself and start coming in awareness. Watch your words. You will stay middle class if you say… 'We are setting a few bucks aside every month, so we can afford the down payment on our dream home.' Or if you are focused on comfort, saying 'I don't want to be rich. I just want to be comfortable.'

The rich use the vocabulary found in the asset column. The rich are rich because they are not focused on comfort and the acquisition of liabilities using credit, as the middle class are. The rich are rich because they focus on the long-term acquisition of assets… assets such as stocks, bonds, system-based businesses and income producing real estate. Many times the rich will forsake meals, a steady pay check, a vacation, or the comfort of a nice home, to build or acquire real assets."

Hari was on a roll! "Here's how a Canadian teacher-couple I know stated it in their personal middle-class-to-rich story…

I quote 2 gems of their exemplary advice…" and saying so he pulled out a folder with a printed email in it.

"If you're a renter looking for a new place, don't just accept what the market has to offer. Instead, put the word out about your good qualities. Great tenants are hard to find. My wife and I placed an ad in the local paper stating that we were two responsible teachers looking for a quality long-term rental. We mentioned the price we'd pay and the exact specifications we sought. Another teacher answered the ad, and offered her place for $180 per month less than nearby apartments. That saved us more than $8,000 over four years - equivalent to a $12,000 pre-tax bonus.'

Notice what they focused on? Their Assets… Themselves!

'Low-cost index funds beat most actively managed mutual funds over the long haul. So when financial planners try to put you into an actively managed fund, tell them thanks, but no. Sure, you might get lucky and pick an actively managed fund that does beat the market, but it's nearly impossible to pick winners ahead of time. Looking at past performance doesn't help: the top performing funds of one decade usually lag in the next decade. Pick a guru who buys and holds stocks for long periods (so you don't end up buying after the guru has sold) then emulate what he's doing. Warren Buffett would be my choice. His most recent large investments have been in Anheuser-Busch and Wal-Mart. Once you buy, hold on and be patient.'

Once again, their focus has been to follow the rich on asset-linked investments."

"Nice examples of a left to right quadrant shift. Did you contact these people online?" I checked.

"Yes, " said Hari and the discussion floated on…

Now as I was discovering during this time, the internet was a great place to get in a rich neighborhood or make rich friends. Why? Because many forums, and facebook too, housed communities of rich-minded people. And entry for anyone was on par. So it was easier to snap out of the middle class and 'decide to be rich'.

Network with successful business owners . Watch what they do. Ask questions earnestly. Emulate. And be on the way!

With the imminent social change network marketing is set to bring, it is the middle class mindset that will dissolve. Kiyosaki warns of this often and emphatically states that network marketing provides for self-reliance.

I believe 'self' is the key word here. Gandhi said, 'be the change you want to see in this world'. 62 years after he left the planet, few people remain inspired to do so. All successful network marketers do, however. And the belief spreads as you meet them at the ever-growing meetings in every corner of the globe.

And shortly we would see them at my B-quadrants' institution. I was convinced I had it there. As belief spreads, hope rises. And hope is the springboard for possibility thinking in a new orbit. The orbit we are moving humanity into.

Teamwork, Trust and Training

Mahesh was standing at a white board, excited as Donald Duck, as he animatedly spoke about sportsmen. We were about 10 of us sprawled all over his living room on a summer Sunday morning. This was the one room in which he could let his hair down. He could bring his inner child out and speak of his dreams and nobody would smirk.

He had once wanted to be a professional sportsman and found professional networking came as close to that as was possible… because it is also about internal development and external well being. Because it also got ordinary folks to earn the kind of money Tiger Woods, Michael Jordan, Sachin Tendulkar, Pele or Adam Gilchrist did. Because it also relied heavily on teamwork, rather than individual expertise.

"But Mahesh, Tiger Woods is an individual expert," someone objected.

Behind his corporate mahogany table Mahesh's life was different. Nobody would challenge him outright that way. People revered him for his business acumen and shuddered at his no-nonsense ways.

He liked that life too. But it was not getting him to his real goal. It was keeping him busy all right. "You want to be busy to be busy, or you want to busy to be free?" Asim often asked. This line suddenly flashed across my mind, as I wondered whether Tiger was busy or free when he played. And Mahesh replied.

"Tiger Woods? Do you even have a clue how many people are on his team? His caddy is one you see. A great source of mental energy. His coach, dietician, hairdresser... many more. In fact he needs his personal entourage because he can't be seen at a barber shop. That's the price you pay to be a celebrity... and you handle the attitudes and expectations of each person on your team... or you may not have the right attitude to be a world champ yourself."

"Point taken boss."

"Same goes for any sportsman. If the skirt-stylist gets half-percent off the mark, the mental agony that would create in Serena Williams' mind could cost her the US Open!" Mahesh continued. "If Michael Schumacher's tire-fitters took a fraction of a second longer than expected they could cause millions of dollars of practice and pain to go down the tube. Do we regard our teams with that ferocity? Are we really networking with the championship spirit? These are questions you have to ask yourselves..."

Suddenly I felt relieved that in network marketing I would have the money and none of the accompanying pain. Comparatively, networking was very forgiving. And I would have the time to pursue my real passions. If I could have an asset churn the money for me, I figured I could charge whatever I felt like as fee at my consulting company. Something I couldn't have done ever in my 20 years of professional life. If I chose, I could offer it for free. Or to celebrities only. It didn't matter. I was not going to be dependent on my ability for my income. For my survival. I could live a life of no compromise. That was thrilling.

"Moreover boss, I read somewhere, Tiger started playing golf at age 2 and it took him 13 years to be an international celebrity. Isn't it silly people expect to be loaded overnight when they step into network marketing?" someone else remarked.

"Well, I don't" Mahesh quickly clarified. "Do you?" I would have loved to say yes. The excitement of stepping into a get-rich-quick option was great. But I found myself saying a very emphatic "No" as I joined a chorus.

"Most people crash and burn within 48 hours of getting into network marketing because of this. They think they have the panacea and everybody they know must agree with them. But other people don't get it. Just as they don't get anything new instantly. And that's why newcomers must tread along the path directed by their team. Networking can't be done alone. Sounds obvious, but people simply miss that point," Mahesh went on.

It was like something inside him was afire. He was in his element that morning.

Srinivas added, "They take it on as a hobby. Try it for a while to see what happens. Nothing happens. A professional income of a few hundred thousand a year or a business income of a few million doesn't arise out of a hobby mentality, does it?"

I found myself getting angry at this… as prospects who gave me a hard time with this one flashed across the screen of my mind. I was in awareness of myself. Happy again.

According to scientific research, the brain fires 60,000 thought signals everyday. How many of these do we really get a chance to catch? And act upon? Why not be selective and stay with only those thoughts that will positively contribute to our preferred future? Would the death toll from yesterday's plane crash matter to us in any way? If it would just serve as a tea party conversation, can't we think of being the messenger of more positive conversation?

If we immerse ourselves in positive thought, ideas and association, wouldn't we always have a subject to speak on? Can't we speak of positivity alone? I believe the time has come for this to take a significant spot in our social interaction. And a wonderful side effect of this happening will be a significant growth in trust. Negativity always sucks away trust.

As if stealing from my mind Shekhar said, "Trust is the cornerstone of any serious endeavor. Marriages last on trust. Sales occur because of trust. People take an action only when they trust that the action will bring the result they desire. Otherwise they simply dabble as they would in a hobby."

I silently discovered was at the same word on a different plane. Words take on different meanings based on the orbit one operates in. I felt compelled to tender my point…

"Shekhar the more people start trusting this simple business, the more positivity there will be in society."

"How?"

"Well, that's what they will talk about. And that will result in more social proof of networking and the positive, dream-oriented conversations it brings about." I said

"And the more such conversations, the more it will be established as acceptable in society."

"Which in turn will result in more trust about the virtue of investing time with positivity," I continued, enjoying the upward spiral I was creating with Shekhar.

"Which will lead to a higher consciousness of individuals …"

"Which will manifest in society as a whole." I found myself articulating, as a rather utopian approach to the growth of civilization… but that was sincerely how I felt.

Mahesh too had thoughts on this. "The 2010-2020 decade is significant for humankind because new levels of trust are expected to arise. Has anyone read 'The Speed of Trust' by Mark Covey?" Unfazed by the silence, he continued, "The rise of consciousness and enormity of literature being developed in the early 21st century on this issue gives every reason to perceive this as the time for massive trust to take over."

Network marketing thrives on trust. It has been maligned by untrustworthy operators who have made their quick buck. But as in any industry past the formative stage, a shakeout is happening in network marketing as well. The wave of trust that the new networking leadership can usher into the world can well precipitate the metamorphosis of the human race at large.

*****

To the outsider, this entire episode might appear crazy. It would have appeared so to me, a few years ago. So I do understand how that feels. But as you have journeyed with me so far into this book, let me ask you, "how will it hurt you to get to the bottom of this?" I mean how exactly will it hurt? Will you have a time challenge to associate with positive people? Will you have an ego challenge in accepting that there's stuff you really know nothing about? Or will you be afraid to remove the mask of self-importance you wear till you die?

Do you see, by asking these questions I am merely nudging you into a greater awareness of yourself. That's step one to living to your full potential. Being in awareness of your thoughts and emotions. So trust. And participate in the creation of a better world for our kids. Talk to a network marketer today.

*****

"And this is exactly why we must focus on the Training guys" said Mahesh back in his sportsman role. "Network marketing is not an obvious business. Because it takes place on the inside. The outer manifestation – as a few thousand people on a strategically designed network – is no big deal. Any corporation can put together such teams in minutes, with a single inter-office memo. The issue in network marketing is that nobody gets paid just to fall in line. People naturally operate from an employee mentality. The fear of 'not falling in line' drives them. A 'takers' attitude. We only volunteer to follow our dreams for a bit… and in the absence of any tangible result, we stop trusting. But if we don't stop… like the business owners who invest in the development of their systems don't stop… we will be yanked out of the 'takers' attitude and plugged into the 'givers' mindset."

"Will that be a permanent shift?" Asiya asked, internally stirred by something.

Asiya was one of my early partners who I'd imagined would replicate my Malaysian experience in India. Burka-clad, ambitious and ready to fight for freedom. Only, nothing till then had stirred anything in her. It was making me cry, but that was how life was.

"It may take time depending on the extent of baggage the person carries from their past, but the shift is definite. When it happens, you'll be thrilled," replied Mahesh.

That was a message for me. I found myself smiling involuntarily.

"I can think of an example in what I do", said Vijender. "A few years back, as President of the Rotary I found I was leading a pack of volunteer members. Each had his own agenda, and life to lead, but we were all voluntarily together in the Rotary for social good. I had a dream that in my year of Presidency I would build drinking water projects in fifty villages. To organize everything to make that happen called for enormous strength from inside me but that was also exactly what made that one year of Presidency so rewarding for me."

"Exactly Vij", I said as I recalled that year he won our trust and focused us on his vision. "Which was why so many of us made those far-our trips to the villages. Can you do the same for your family's dreams? Your network will respond the same way you know."

"You mean they will think of my family's all-expenses-paid vacation in Bahamas the same way as they'd think of a drinking water project?"

"No, not really. But they will see that you believe that the vehicle you both are on will carry you to your dreams and thus it will carry them to theirs. The transference of belief is the same."

Nand interjected, "Isn't this where the difference between individual vision and collective vision come in? How will it work?"

"Let me ask you this Vijender... you said that Rotary year was rewarding... why?" I asked planning to answer the question by deflecting it.

"I learned a lot. Felt I grew."

"How?"

"Leadership I guess. Until that year I was merely managing my factory. From that year on I was able to lead my team through delegation and commission three new plants as well."

"Wow! If that's what being pushed into leadership can do to you in one year, imagine what it would be like as a way of life. Three factories are like 3 teams – or 3 showrooms as Mahesh would put it – each with its own quirks!"

Nand mused. "So then Sandeep why don't most network marketing biggies set up large businesses on the side?"

I couldn't help laughing out loud. "Why Nand, they do! You've heard of the huge social benefit organizations Jim Dornan, Doug Wead, Jay Kubassek, Beverly Sallee and so many others head up. Guess it makes sense to leave industry to the folks who'd rather not enjoy their true freedom. Besides, training is a huge industry. My dream is to build the world's first B-quadrant training institute and that will take a lot of ground work, training and resource mobilization, which I am doing right now as we build our networks."

Nand, typically pensive at 58, reflected, "we spend the first 20 years of our lives training for the next 60. If only we kept voluntarily training ourselves in parallel we could do so much course correction."

"And avoid the mid-life crisis around 40, when we realize we are not where we wanted to be and have no clue why," added Vijender.

That last comment jolted me a bit. In fact it took me back to the plane I was boarding, returning from Malaysia. I too had had a dream... to retire at 40... and that was round the corner... and I wasn't close. Was I heading for a crisis? That was when, on the flight, Nama had popped the question...

So where are we headed?

The flight from Kuala Lumpur to Hyderabad was very much on time. Made me wonder if 'late flights' were purely an Indian phenomenon. Back home, it seemed so normal to have to wait, that one actually budgeted time for it.

As we huddled across the aerobridge Nama and Tharini caught up with me. They had been enjoying a cozy coffee. I had declined in favor of some extra reading. 'The Courage To Succeed', by a 3-time Olympian Ruben Gonzalez. There were many lessons to learn from sportspersons… especially from serious Olympians. The network marketing game is played on the inside. Abundance is a mindset… as is winning.

"What was your dream in college Sandeep?" Nama had asked as we settled down next to each other on the flight. We both had aisle seats and that gave me enough privacy to read or talk as I chose. At that moment we were into the JB spirit (no pun intended). Nama had no clue about how well defined my dream had become in those past few days… he was just starting at the start.

"To retire by 40. I've desired that since college… but life happened and it had stopped looking feasible till now" I confessed.

"Life happened." Nama repeated. "Did you know life is a balance of 3 key things that each living being must master. And these three things are not biology, psychology and mathematics... which we painstakingly learn. These are Nature, Wealth and Empowerment."

"Huh?"

"Yes, your Success depends on what you do with Nature, Wealth and Empowerment, and each lies in abundance in network marketing." Nama continued authoritatively. "Nature refers to the preservation and growth of all that we are. The Body, Mind, Emotion, Thought and Spirit."

"What is the connection?" I asked, seeming to miss the point totally.

"Well, if retiring was your definition of success, that was just a state of mind, which is driven by nature... plus wealth, because you need money to retire on... and empowerment, because someone you've trained needs to hold the baton you pass... else you can't retire. The same is true of any success."

"Tell me more Nama... this is tangential," I said, suddenly perked up like a 4-year old before his grandma at bedtime.

"Well," Nama obliged with a smile. Secretly he'd been wanting to share this nugget all along for it was a great way to structure success. "In our context, the body is the grossest form of nature. It is the tangible. The obvious. And practically, quite useless. For example let's imagine our body is like ice. You can feel it, hold it, lug it around, but it is mostly a liability. To make an asset of it, one has to work to make it subtler. Like a gymnast or ballerina… their bodies are subtle, light… and like good assets, put money into their pockets. Remember what Robert Kiyosaki says about assets and liabilities?"

"Sure, I'm with you… assets put money in the pocket. Liabilities take money out of the pocket" I beamed.

"That being the case, would you agree that there's a difference between a mechanic and a sculptor?" I nodded. "Would you also agree that the sculptor is more of a creator than the mechanic? And that the creator is the one closer to nature than the other?" I nodded again. "If so, think about this… vis-a-vis your body, your doctor is a mechanic whereas you are the sculptor. And this is what the 'wellness' industry is all about, as opposed to 'sickness'. The less you rely on the doctor for your body, the closer you get to whatever you want on this plane."

"Ooo… far out… So how do you stop subscribing to the sickness industry of doctors, hospitals, and pharmacies?" I asked.

"By subscribing to the wellness industry of health coaches, gyms and organic supplements! You have to subscribe to one or the other… might as well make prevention better than cure! Though you may spend 5 times more on organic supplementation than you do on synthetic vitamins, minerals, and omega3s, you must know that by ingesting chemicals you are only fooling yourself… you're not taking your body much closer to nature." Nama continued emphatically. "And remember your body is turned on by natural surroundings, so take time to deliberately get close to them… water your plants, holiday in the hills, walk in the park… you owe it to you!"

"Pretty good." I was wondering about the other parts of nature by this time. The mind… yes, retirement was a matter of the mind… and of the body too, come to think of it.

As though he were reading my thoughts, Nama continued, "if the body was ice, the mind is water. It can go anywhere. Glide better than a ballerina over anything. And it can even cut through rock… making it quite powerful. So obviously, 'naturalizing' the mind calls for a higher degree of determination and skill, right?"

"Right!"

"I found a simple, practical way of doing this by looking at where the mind manifested its monkeydom the most. And you know what I found? It was in fuelling the ego. The mind is the 'I'," a triumphant Nama declared.

"But how can we consciously reduce the ego?" I asked innocently.

"By looking into our relationships. Ego does not work in isolation. It always needs a partner. There are a few great books that will help set this right for you, based on proven principles of relationships and visualization. The mind feeds on words. The words you use; the self-talk you indulge in; the benchmarks you set; can either propel you to achieve what you want… or equally easily detract you from getting there. Be careful what you say. Mean it fully or don't say it.

Again, don't fool yourself… you will only sabotage your oneness with nature."

"So the recourse lies in books? They will take me where the authors have been… to lead the life I dream to lead?" I felt a cynic rising in me, questioning the commerce of all this. But then I said to myself, calm down… it's only your ego. Accept this and be open and willing to take small steps… they will not hurt you.

Oblivious of my thoughts Nama continued, "The mind is like a garden. We plant into it the weeds of murder, deception, rape, ignominy from the daily newspaper and expect roses to blossom. Is there a chance? Switch off your TV, cancel the paper. You will still know what you need to, while you read these books and move to the next level of oneness!"

"And what's that?"

"Emotion. Moving from the 'conscious' mind, we are now attempting to tame the 'subconscious' mind. This is where emotions reside. Numerous studies, including Dr. Glen Doman's extensive research on children, reveal beyond doubt that more than 80% of everything we learn is permanently hardwired in our minds before the age of 6. Scary, isn't it? Even before we learn how to spell 'knife' we intuitively know that a knife is an object of 'fear'. And it takes a lot of undoing to remove that instinctive emotion of fear and replace it with a 'love' for the knife… which is why many of us carelessly cut ourselves. This arises from the fear vibration. Why would anything we love harm us?"

"Whatever you resist, will persist" I pronounced trying to edge in something intelligent myself. Many people quote these wise words and I did too. Getting into emotional oneness with nature – like with the mind – is about getting into a state of acceptance. Being open and willing to 'not resist' and instead 'go with the flow' so that all the obstacles to what we want can be washed away just like water washes through rock.

Just then the airhostess started to announce flight safety rules and we sat upright in mock attention. It gave me a few minutes to ruminate over all I had been hearing.

I realized the subconscious was far far bigger than the conscious. So the extent of work required to 'accept' was also far far bigger. And this was why emotional triggers such as "creative visualization" and "vision boards" were useful to direct our emotions towards where we really wanted to be. The power of these tools was enormous and though they appeared childish, were not. Now that the context was clear, I decided to search up resources for these and practice the techniques in conjunction with whatever I did for my mind and body. What could be the next thing I wondered?

Obviously the 'unconscious' area of the mind. Or thought. If the mind was the brain, and emotion the 'heart', thought was the 'gut'. Yes. The umbilical cord connects to the gut. Everything we know about everything from this life and the previous one/s we know in our unconscious. And that's why thought drives decisions faster than any other force. Thought is the subtlest form of the mind and therefore can reach inter-galactical and unimagined areas in a jiffy… something the body or the ego would never be able to do.

I can think a Mercedes Benz into reality. It just calls for an acute level of oneness of mind, heart and gut with nature. Working on thought can therefore be immensely rewarding... but for this we must appreciate its power and prioritize time to address its needs.

Fortunately, the 'needs' of thought are not many. In fact just one. And that is to be in awareness. To know at every moment what one is doing. To be in the 'now'. To watch what we see... to watch what we say... to watch what we take in. Again I was reminded of the burka-clad women of the previous day. They were in sheer oneness.

As humans, we are experts at being in the past or in the future. The choice to keep oneness with thought is ours. Great sportspersons do just this. There is no other thought in their heads as they dash the 100 meters. Asafa Powell, the fastest man in the world and ambassador for Nutrilite would endorse this. For those of you who have seen 'The Last Samurai', a 2-word advice from the highly disciplined Japanese says all you'd need know about winning... "No mind."

By now the airhostess was gone and we could talk again. "Hey Nama was 'thought' the next one you'd mentioned?"

"Yes... did you figure it or was that from memory?"

"I was just thinking... it flows so logically... in fact the book 'The Secret' speaks so much about the oneness of Thought with Nature. Louise Hay and several others have replaced medicine with thought cures. This is big Nama. It is an unexplained science and our talking about this is taking us into that level of consciousness required to fathom more."

"I agree. You know this story of the ant and the elephant?" Nama asked.

"No, tell me."

"Well, it's a long and interesting one about this ant that lived on an elephant's back. The summary is that the ant was representative of our conscious minds, in terms of size and capability, and the elephant it resided on represented the subconscious emotions and unconscious thoughts. Now the ego of the mind believed it was traveling west... but because the elephant was going east, like it or not, the ant was going east too!"

"Ha, ha" that was vivid, I thought as I laughed. "We are mostly like the ants... victims of our circumstances."

"And the B-quadrant brings us out of victim mode and into limitlessness, which we are often unprepared for" chimed Nama equally pleased as he went on... "because this is where the most subtle part of our existence comes in. The 'steam' from our water analogy."

I visualized steam as the powerful force that moved locomotives; that scarred planets; that transformed elements from one to another. "And that is the Spirit!" I exclaimed with raised eyebrows, "oneness with the divine is the level at which the spirit probably operates, doesn't it?"

"Yes, though for it to operate effectively, it requires a oneness of the others with nature. But nature is very accommodating. Just don't push it. We must align ourselves non-religiously but spiritually through any doctrine that works for us. The spirit is the ultimate form of nature and oneness with it is the purity we are born with. To stay with the child-like innocence and to love the child within us are means to this end. Ultimately it is about aligning your energy centers with the universe."

"You mean the chakras? I asked.

"Yes."

"But why is it important to align these five?"

"Because that enables us to tap into oneness with life. Remember it's life we're talking about? Retirement and all that?" Nama smiled earnestly.

"Hmmm… and the next is oneness with wealth, right?"

"Yes! Oneness with wealth ensures we get our inner barometer in synch with external impulses. The signals we generate and receive through our lives and interactions are exchanged through money. Like you know water finds its own level? So do we, based on our ideas of money."

I had thought about this earlier, while thinking of energy. In energy terms also, money was water. Just as water found its own level, so did we, in whatever society we chose. Water leaked. So did money. I had actually studied my relationship with water (I mean really pondered over it) and resolved some money issues magically. For instance, once I was in awareness of the connection, I always attended to leaky taps around the house promptly!

What's more, I had figured that the one essential requirement for success to manifest, was to be part of a B-quadrant support group. This was no big discovery. Spiritual enhancement happened in support groups like 'Art of Living'. Mental enhancement happened in support groups like 'Mensa'. Physical enhancement happened in support groups like 'Gyms and wellness centers'. Emotional enhancement happened in support groups like 'Alcoholics Anonymous'. Social enhancement happened in support groups like 'Rotary Clubs'. So why would things be different when it came to Financial enhancement? Money would find its own level after all.

"Yes Nama, I get this. Wealth equal to success is easy to understand anyway and associating with wealthy mindsets makes it possible. What about empowerment?"

"Empowerment is about impact. Contribution. Purpose. Why are we occupying place on this planet? What are we doing for others? How are we transferring our uniqueness to society at large… or just to our kids… or even to our neighbors, friends and domestic help? What makes us important in this world is our ability to empower others. And the key factors for healthy empowerment include integrity, ethics and peaceful demeanor."

"Right Sir! Reminds me of the story of the young man and his son who were on a bus and he bought two tickets. The ticket collector said, "it's ok to buy one… kids below five are permitted free and nobody would guess that your kid is over 5." "That's ok", the man replied, "give me 2 tickets because my son knows he's over 5," I narrated.

"Absolutely… that is a valuable lesson in empowerment. This kid would form permanent mental equations about a lot of aspects in his life through that episode. Self-worth, self-esteem, truth, compromise, money, abundance consciousness, ethics, justice… all this from his dad's basic integrity to himself," Nama thought out loud.

"And so, even before they got off the bus they would have impacted the world in a sense. The kid may grow up to become the President of the United Nations. And he'd operate from this very paradigm!" I added.

"Empowerment actually has 2 components… Leadership and consciousness." Nama went on to explain. "The funny thing about leadership is that it is obviously not taught in 'management' school. Yet managers think they know it instinctively."

I laughed! "Management and Leadership are subjects of the left and the right quadrants respectively and that's what unlearning and relearning in the corporate world should all be about."

"Sure, managers are given numerous hours of leadership training, but by whom? Not by leaders. But by other employees who have only read more and made more schematic diagrams in the wrong quadrant!" said Nama with a smile as he paused to accept the refreshments the in-flight executive had brought us.

"So who is a leader?" Nama questioned rhetorically as he crackled some chips with gusto. "A leader is one who can empower others. In doing so, he or she inspires, envisions and works up a team. Nobody can make anyone else work for their selfish motives. They could enslave at one time, but not anymore."

"So how does one empower?" I asked.

"Through my mentors in Network Marketing I have learnt that it takes 3 Es," Nama said. "Envisioning, Edifying and Energizing."

"Envisioning is the root of inspiration. For instance if Cortez could not have shared the vision, he might have 'managed' a trip like the others did... but not led a victorious voyage. Since the crew could envision the treasure for themselves, they were inspired."

"Hmmm... and edifying?"

"Edifying is a strong underlying team-building principle. Edification is loosely like 'passing the ball' - in football - by speaking well of and building up people on the team, especially leaders. What it does is, it creates an upward spiral of positivity across the rank and file of the team, which sucks entire communities into its powerful spin. An example is how NASA and JFK edified each other to result in a man on the moon!"

"Yes, I remember ..." I interrupted, "Doug Wead often said, you can promote anyone and anything in the world except yourself. As the President's right hand man he would know!"

"Correct," Nama continued, "and energizing is what Churchill and Gandhi and Mao and Lenin have done with their famous words that manifested revolutions. A leader stirs up an energy that empowers. And this oneness with empowerment is what creates the leverage that enables work of the magnitude impossible for any single human being!"

That was a lot to munch on. But Nama was on a roll.

"While leadership would be the commercial way to understand oneness with empowerment, spiritually it is the surrender to a higher power that makes the impossible possible."

"But," I interrupted again, trying to understand the nuances, "this higher power has first to be empowered by the self, or the ego... by submitting itself... right?"

"Quite true Sandeep, much like the leader has to take a servant position and let the team create victories of epic proportions," Nama clarified through analogy. "It is not surprising therefore that we always hear of 'spiritual leaders' and never of 'spiritual managers'." We both laughed!

"As you observe B-quadrant leaders – like successful network marketers – you'll be astounded to note the remarkably higher consciousness they operate from. Did you figure that?"

"Oh yes, for sure!"

"Look for their knee-jerk reactions. Impulsive reflexes. They will always be extraordinary... always thinking of the other person, not themselves. And this is because such people have designed their lives using empowerment principles. On the abundance side. Demonstrating Oneness with Nature , Wealth and Empowerment. Which are the keys to Success."

"Is this about success in network marketing alone or success in general?" I asked.

"The fact that Success is a function of oneness with Nature, Wealth and Empowerment is a general life principle Sandeep. You know, there was this champion golfer... I forget his name... who was accosted by a woman outside the club and she told him she had a dying baby and needed help. The golfer on impulse handed his day's winnings over to her. The next week someone told him that that woman was a fraud and he had got taken in... and you know what his instant response was?"

"No, what?"

"Oh wow, that's great news... so there's no dying baby you mean!" said Nama with equanimity. "That, my friend, is the mark of a truly successful person... who operates from a deep spiritual connection, abundant wealth and a forever-giving and forgiving attitude... get it?"

"Wow!" That was all I could articulate. Nama had been through everything I had in the last couple of months several times over. No wonder he spoke like a diamond himself. Wow.

*****

As I pushed my seat back and reclined for the long haul, my thoughts returned to what success meant to me. It was important to know this clearly... because we can't get to a place that we do not define. Like one can't buy a ticket for a journey when one doesn't know one's destination.

The key to achieving success therefore lies in defining it. And that was where Nama's original question had came from... In my initial startup Mahesh had mentioned, "to pin-point your dream, think of what you imagined life would be when you were a child of five... you may have thought you'd be a fireman, or a doctor, a pilot or something exciting like that. Quite unlikely a manager or an accountant... but look at how many of us have wound up that way!"

Obviously he was joking, but his point was, we must revisit the impressions we create in our early years. Those were on an empty canvas, free of pre-conceived ideas of what was possible and what was not. In senior school, we might have imagined a big house, a fancy car, a respectable position, a magical spouse... and we may have rationalized that it was 'not our thing' by the time we got into work life. Or even if we had found a magical spouse (like I had), we'd create something to sabotage ourselves (like I did... I am still figuring out why... and that's what my next book is on.)

And then, for some of us, the mid-life crisis comes! And that's when we cement in our minds, our reduced definition of success... which we'd arrived at with completely inadequate knowledge of 'how to achieve' success anyway. To achieve is not taught anywhere... in school, home or at work. And that's why the crisis arises.

But actually, let's face it, those are our dreams. The ones in early life. And it is never too late – or too early – to start to pursue them.

Mahesh had also shared with me a card on which were 8 goals that people typically picked, when asked 'what would you want in life':

a/ Extra income (to buy the cars, houses, travel the world…)
b/ Financial freedom (when income through assets is greater than expenses)
c/ Good health
d/ More time with family
e/ Personal development & relationships
f/ To be able to give to others
g/ Recognition
h/ To leave a legacy

"You can pick one of these too," he had urged me, "and flesh it out in greater detail. For instance, Recognition might mean an excellence award for you at work. Now think deep… Which award? Why would that be important? What skills would you need to win it? Where would you need to go for the skills? Who would mentor you? Would it require extra time/ money/ health/ relationships/ grace/ or a combination of these? (There can be no other requirement). Where will that come from? How will you feel when you get recognized? I mean how will you really FEEL? What vibrations will your inner self emit? And so on… meditate on these aspects till you can actually attract that to you!"

*****

Thanks to the journey I took, making network marketing a way of life, I came upon this true purpose of my being. I had unveiled my dreams, strengths and passions. With them firmly in place all events and people started manifesting in my life like a divine cosmic dance. And life got exciting as never before.

Could one have identified one's purpose and derived fulfillment by other means? Of course! Certainly! But none would have produced this result alongside one's existing activity. Alongside one's pre-set evolving definition of comfort; without doing anything out of the ordinary. It may seem like I speak utopia, but if progressive change is what we want, network marketing is the natural way to grow into it.

"It's just small steps", Nama was saying sometime later on the flight back from Malaysia, "like a baby trying to walk... when she falls it's not the end of her attempts. She sees everyone on their two feet and realizes it's possible. So she gets up and tries again. You and I have to create that social proof for everyone in the world to be able to walk as a network marketer. I see you are getting stronger now."

It must have shone in my eyes. The eyes are the mirror of the mind. "Yes Nama, this meeting did me a lot of good. Thank you."

"Ah, the attitude of gratitude. It is so fundamental to success and yet so underrated." He was so right. I was so very grateful to have been taught the right things to do at the right time. To have been open to learn... I am thankful. I could have been living a life of quiet desperation, silently passing away my existence, oblivious of the possibilities I now exercise.

As the sun parked itself atop the Hyderabad horizon I could sense that we were descending. The sky flirted with every color from orange to purple as we rocketed towards the ground. A dull thud and mild screech told us we were home. We had landed. I had taken off.

Appendix 1

The Vibratory Scale Of Consciousness

Originally I had planned to reproduce the scale exactly the way David R. Hawkins, M.D., Ph.D., had presented it in his book Power v/s Force, but his agents felt it would be an infringement on copyright. So I have here the next best option... please search 'Map of Consciousness' on the internet and look up the exact scale.

For a preliminary understanding I must share that the Vibratory Levels range from 25 to 1000, based on his involuntary muscle-movement studies. Each Level corresponds with a particular Emotion and a corresponding State of being. For instance the Levels 25, 50 and 75 correspond with the Emotions of 'humiliation, blame and despair' resulting in the States of 'shame, guilt and apathy' respectively. Imagine a world vibrating there... how terrible that would be!

As we go through rising States of 'grief, fear, desire, anger and pride' we reach a Level of 200, where the Emotion is 'affirmation' and the State is 'courage'. That's approximately where the world lies currently... with an optimistic hope for the future. Moving higher through the States of 'willingness, acceptance, reason, love and joy', at 'peace' we hit the 600 mark of Emotional 'bliss'. And beyond that is the 700-1000 band of 'ineffable' Emotions that are found in the elusive State of 'enlightenment'.

Consciousness In Network Marketing

I am not sure where the origin of the Paradigm Theory lies but I suspect it is in the book 'A Course in Miracles'... since the thread is common to Colin Tipping (Radical Manifestation) and Bijan (Effortless Prosperity), both students of the 'Course'. I've taken the paradigms from the 'Experiential Guide To The Celestine Prophecy' and added the third column from my experience with network marketing. It was these realizations which in fact banged me well and proper into the network marketing industry!

By way of a prelude put simply, the essential difference between the old and new paradigms is:

Old: We are human beings who have spiritual experiences

New: We are spiritual beings who have human experiences

Now, with this slight shift in perspective, everything of how we view the world, religion, politics, business and parenting among other things, changes. Dramatically.

And creating successful network marketers is probably the most effective way of empowering individuals in the way of the new paradigm. Here's why:

Old Paradigm	New Paradigm	Relationship with Network Marketing
Independence	*Inter-dependence*	*A network is disconnected by independence. Interdependence is the key to build one*
Intellectual accomplishment	*Wisdom*	*Networks are B-quadrant and rely on cumulative wisdom. Intellect is an individual S-quadrant trait*
Self-criticism	*Acknowledge strengths*	*Network marketers operate in close knit teams that acknowledge and leverage each other's strengths*
Security	*Adaptability*	*Network marketing necessitates an openness and deep desire to change, which calls for adaptability*
Resistance to authority	*Sharing leadership*	*Success in network marketing is achieved by creating leaders and sharing the mantle*
Emotional dramas	*Self-actualization*	*Any B-quadrant business is built with a purpose beyond the self. Especially network marketing*
Fear	*Love*	*Networking being a people's business calls for deep-rooted love for all, to achieve success*
Control	*Trust*	*In a network you lead an army of 'volunteers'. Trust is key. Only a 'paid' army can be controlled*
Gaining approval	*Self-trust*	*Networking being leadership-driven mandates the leader to have self-trust and to keep walking*

Conformity	*Creativity*	*Network marketing is a non-conformist way of intellectual distribution by definition*
Family entanglements	*Honest commitments*	*A networker can not keep two faces if success is the long-term goal. Period*
Addictions	*Self-security*	*Self-security about oneself, one's team and the companies associated with are critical*
Overspending	*Healing deprivation*	*Overspending is a common reason for failure of networkers. Requires inner healing*
Under-earning	*Being paid what you are worth*	*A very high self-worth (of some) is the reason network marketers have no earning limits*
Physical image	*Intrinsic worth*	*In order to succeed, network marketers need to work on their inner selves, which outweighs all else*
Lack of love	*Divine love within*	*The process of addressing the inner self brings about divine love within*
Anger	*Empowerment*	*The process of building teams and leadership rests on quality empowerment*
Guilt	*Love with wisdom*	*"Have no regrets"… principle #1 for network marketers. Naturally there is no place for guilt*
Perfectionism	*Self-acceptance*	*B-quadrant networking is all about 'not being the expert' and accepting the system*
Revenge	*Forgiveness*	*The easiest way to kill a network marketing business is to think small (vengefulness)*

How much money you can make is dependent not on what business you build but rather on how big you build your mind. Is your mental crucible large enough to hold a few billion dollars, or would it only fit a few thousand?

Are you saying the right things to yourself? The excuse, "I don't have the money", spoken to a network marketing sponsor is self-defeating for life. In saying so, you are programming your brain to 'not have money' and be ok with the idea. Poor choice!

Are you getting the picture here? The money is in your mind. And some good B-quadrant friends can get your mental blueprint about wealth better organized for you.

Now that you know the money is in your mental crucible, here's a game you can play to help you get it from there. It's fun and will surprise you! Be at it for 60 days and watch your crucible expand! Here's the game:

Start a fresh notebook. Turn to page 1. Write down any imaginary figure you are comfortable with, to earn in a day. For example, if you are on a $ 3000 /month salary that's $ 100 per day… but maybe your mind is comfortable even with accepting $ 1000 /day. So write that. Don't write any large figure that your mind will not accept.

Now, the idea is to use this money up on the same page. Below the figure, write what your mandatory expenses are. Groceries, utility payments and loans typically stand at the top of the list. By the time you finish expenses, be sure you end on a zero balance.

Next day, again put an earnings figure on top of page 2. This figure must be equal to or greater than the previous day's. Again, apportion expenses. Once you've finished with recurring needs, look at the longer term expenses... like the house loan... pay off more than just a month's installment. Next, look at non-mandatory expenses you've been budgeting for... the holiday in India for instance... and again, end the page on zero balance.

On the third day, once more, put an earning figure on top of page 3. Obviously this figure must be equal to or greater than the previous day's. Again, apportion expenses. Do this till you can't think of any other thing you need to spend money on... except luxuries. In case you finish expenses, tithe a little (give to charity). The tithing amount should be no greater than 10% of the reminder. Over? Spend some on luxuries till you reach a zero balance.

Next day, again put a figure equal to or greater than the previous day's on top of page 4. Give yourself a bigger hike. Continue with immediate expenses first, long-term next, non-mandatory after that, a little tithing, a little luxury. Chances are you will get to this point after many more days than 4, but for sake of this example let's imagine you're done now and still have money left over. Now start investing the remainder. Invest in assets. Check prices of gold, property, mutual funds... see how much the remainder of your money can buy.

Remember Robert Kiyosaki 's sound anti-depression advice, "the rich put money into assets, not expenses". So continue doing this. Be sure to have a big smile on your face everyday as you start writing into your notebook.

Also make sure you have no money left over on every page. Put a bit aside for necessities everyday. Pay off all your debts. Enjoy all the luxuries you can imagine and gift and tithe and invest alongside (in that order).

Play this game sincerely till you reach page 60 and watch what it does to your mind. I guarantee you will be on your way to being abundantly, happily rich! And this might be the time to start taking your sponsor and your business really seriously... because unlike every traditional business, the online / network marketing money vehicle operates with absolutely no limits – except your mind!

"You are not really wealthy if you can count how much money you make" – Jim Dornan

Appendix 4
Identifying Life Purpose

Here's an exercise to start to arrive at your mission. I'd like you to pull out 3 white papers.

On the first one, write down as many bulleted points as you can, about 'What your strengths are'. These are personality traits or acquired skills.

On the second one write down as many bulleted points as you can, about 'What you are passionate about'. These are things that make your heart feel happy.

On the third one write down the biggest things that come to your mind, about 'What you dream of'. This / these could be lying buried way inside you... perhaps dreams you had in school or even as a child. Come on, pull them out... it's your paper and only for you to read. It will be fun!

Your investment of your time and emotion on this could possibly be the most meaningful thing you've done till date!

Done?

Now examine every point on sheet one and put a rank against each to indicate how highly you feel about it. For example if you had written your strengths as

- smiling personality
- good at driving
- health conscious

- good conversationalist
- good presenter
- photography

And if you felt that Photography was your strongest point and the fact that you were a Good Conversationalist was second strongest, mark 1 and 2 against them respectively.

Now do the same about you passions on sheet two. Again, some could be similar, like Photography could be a passion too, but maybe 'Caring for street children' would be a passion you wrote that really tugs at your heart. So mark the ranks accordingly.

And finally, select your most vivid dream. Mine, for instance, is speaking before a large 100,000+ audience that's standing in ovation :-) What's yours?

Done? Ready?

Great! Now we shall form a sentence. For the sake of this example, we'll take my dream (though the other points are not mine!). And your sentence would combine the top-ranking thoughts of each sheet. For example:

I am on this planet to...

Take and propagate heart-wrenching pictures of living conditions and rehabilitation of street kids
So that...
The world may stand in acclaim of my contribution to integrating the less privileged with the mainstream

Do it!

Now you will notice that the statement that emerged for you has little to do with the Accountant's job you're doing (perhaps... or whatever). But if you do what came out of that statement, you may never need to be an Accountant (or whatever) ever.

So start shooting pictures... set up a photography blog... join street-kid care groups and spread your work.

Don't worry that you don't have the time. Time will come from the priority passion creates. Just start to do it.

Getting yourself into a support group of like minds will accelerate this hugely. And if that group activity funds you as well, you'd get the time for your mission!

For both time and money, you have my online base at www.b-quadrant.com ... different missions, one platform.

Get it? Now go get it!

About the Author

Sandeep Nath is a success coach and consultant with 27 years experience in branding and marketing. He has been a serial entrepreneur for 21 years, setting up healthy ventures in creative consulting, brand strategy, web design, TV production, advertising, software production, market research, event management, management consulting, entrepreneur development, network marketing & internet marketing. He lives in India in New Delhi. He also lives online at www.SandeepNath.com

If you derived value, please share this book.

You could also send US$ 7 to the author by clicking here:

www.ArriveAtSuccess.com